Will Capitalism Survive?

Herbert Schmertz
Paul Seabury
Alan Reynolds
Michael Novak
Albert Shanker
J. Robert Nelson
Eugene J. McCarthy
Paul Craig Roberts
James Cone
Rita Hauser
Jack Kemp
Herman Kahn

Will Capitalism Survive?

Edited by
Ernest W. Lefever

*A Challenge by Paul Johnson
With Twelve Responses*

**Ethics and Public Policy Center
Georgetown University
Washington, D.C.**

Library of Congress Cataloging in Publication Data:
Main entry under title:
Will capitalism survive?
   Includes an edited version of an address, Has
capitalism a future?   A historian's view, originally
delivered by P. Johnson at the Bank Credit Analyst
Conference in New York, May 1978.
   1.   Capitalism—Addresses, essays, lectures.
2.   Wealth, Ethics of—Addresses, essays, lectures.
I.   Schmertz, Herbert, 1930-   II.   Lefever, Ernest W.
III.   Johnson, Paul, 1928-   Has capitalism a
future?   1979.   IV.   Georgetown University, Washington,
D. C.   Ethics and Public Policy Center
HB501.W559   330.12'2   79-55316
ISBN 0-89633-026-5

$3.00

Contents

Foreword

HIGH-SOUNDING AND EMOTIVE WORDS ending in *ism* lead a turbulent life. They are battered about by the crosscurrents of politics, religion, and ideology. *Ism*-words embrace ideas and aspirations. They fuel causes, provoke conflicts, and soothe consciences. Often they are marching words, almost hypnotic in their effect. They reassure the true believer and confound the outsider.

In our time the two chief ideologies that have moved men and nations are fascism and communism, both virulent versions of totalitarianism. The political systems that came to power in their names have manipulated two other *isms*—nationalism and racism—to galvanize and control their subjects.

Capitalism is another passionate word, evoking widely differing values, loyalties, and attitudes. Unlike fascism and communism it does not define a political system, though both communists and fascists have made strident claims to the contrary. Nevertheless, *capitalism* has become a "cause" word on both sides of the struggle between government by coercion and government by consent. Thus it has been imprisoned in a straitjacket and often invested with meanings that neither logic nor facts can sustain. Capitalism has become a code word that badly needs decoding.

For the great American entrepreneurs of the last century and the small Babbitts of the 1930s, capitalism was a symbol of all that is right with this country. For the Marxists it is the root of all evil and must be destroyed along with the political freedoms that make it possible. For many contemporary Western liberals, capitalism is a wayward stepchild in need of severe restraint, regulation, or reform.

In a recent book Irving Kristol gave "two cheers" for capitalism. In this study Paul Johnson asserts that capitalism—or what he calls industrial capitalism and others prefer to call democratic capitalism—merits at

vii

least two and a half cheers, if not three. Mr. Johnson is a former editor of the influential English weekly *The New Statesman* (1965-70) and an erstwhile Fabian socialist. Since he left the *New Statesman* he has written four books: *Enemies of Society* (1977), *A History of Christianity* (1976), *Elizabeth I: A Study of Power and Intellect* (1974), and *The Offshore Islanders: From Roman Occupation to European Entry* (1972). His seemingly abrupt political metamorphosis has made him a controversial and sought-after speaker on both sides of the Atlantic.

This symposium is based on an address—"Has Capitalism a Future? A Historian's View"—that Johnson gave at the Bank Credit Analyst Conference in New York, May 1978. The address was published in the *Bank Credit Analyst* and is reprinted here in a slightly edited form with the permission of the journal and the author.

In it Johnson makes a succinct and spirited defense of industrial capitalism. "Judged simply by its capacity to create wealth and to distribute it," he says, capitalism "is a phenomenon unique in world history. One could argue that it is the greatest single blessing ever bestowed on humanity." He then cites five dangers that threaten the survival of capitalism: the collectivist bias of Western intellectuals, the influence of the ecological apocalyptics, the assault on the market by big government, the undermining of productivity by trade unions, and the totalitarian (primarily Soviet) threat from without.

Will capitalism survive these threats? "It all depends on the United States," says Johnson. True, West Germany and Japan now have flourishing free-enterprise economies, but they also have "a tradition of state capitalism"; this means that under pressure they "would adapt themselves with surprising speed and readiness to a new collectivist order." Thus Johnson throws down the gauntlet.

We asked eighteen persons from various professions and perspectives to respond to Johnson's challenge. Twelve did: an oil executive, a political scientist, a banker, a political columnist, a labor-union official, a professor of theology, a former U.S. senator, a journalist, a black liberation theologian, an international lawyer, a U.S. congressman, and a futurologist. Alas, no card-carrying economist, historian, or philosopher is included, though each contributor can be regarded as an amateur philosopher of history.

The predictive question, Will capitalism survive?, raises the inescapable moral question, *Should* capitalism survive? And if so, in what form? Fundamentally, the economic-political issue is always a moral issue. It was so treated by Adam Smith in his book *A Theory of Moral Sentiments,* published in 1759. It is so treated by the contributors to this volume.

This collection is one of a series of studies published in the Business and Society project of the Ethics and Public Policy Center. Others currently under way address the ethics of nuclear energy, the churches and multinational corporations, investment in southern Africa, advocacy advertising, and corporate philanthropy. All Center publications are intended to combine empirical analysis with moral reasoning and thus to stimulate thoughtful debate on consequential public issues.

ERNEST W. LEFEVER, *Director*
Ethics and Public Policy Center

September 1979

THE CHALLENGE

PAUL JOHNSON

Has Capitalism a Future?

SEEN AGAINST THE GRAND perspective of history, capitalism is a newcomer. I would date it, in its earliest phase in England, only from the 1780s. We now possess some knowledge of economic systems going back to the early centuries of the third millennium B.C. I could outline, for instance, the economic structure of Egypt under the Old Kingdom, about 2700 B.C. Our knowledge of how civilized societies have organized their economic activities thus covers a stretch of more than 4,600 years. And in only about two hundred of those years has industrial capitalism existed. As a widely spread phenomenon, it is barely one hundred years old.

(Before I go any further, let me define my term: by "capitalism" I mean large-scale industrial capitalism, in which privately financed, publicly quoted corporations, operating in a free-market environment, with the back-up of the private-enterprise money market, constitute the core of the national economy. This is a rather broad definition, but I think it will do.)

The next point to note is the remarkable correlation between the emergence of industrial capitalism and the beginnings of really rapid economic growth. Throughout most of history, growth rates, when we have the statistical evidence to measure them, have been low, nil, or minus. A century of

PAUL JOHNSON, *a former editor of the "New Statesman," is a historian and author. He lives in Iver, near London. This essay was first given as an address to the Bank Credit Analyst Conference held in New York and Bermuda in 1978. It is used by permission of the author and of the "Bank Credit Analyst," published by Monetary Research, Hamilton, Bermuda.*

slow growth might be followed by a century of decline. Societies tended to get caught in the Malthusian Trap: that is, a period of slow growth led to an increase in population, the outstripping of food supplies, then a demographic catastrophe, and the beginning of a new cycle.

There were at least three economic "Dark Ages" in history, in which a sudden collapse of the wealth-making process led to the extinction, or virtual extinction, of civilized living, and the process of recovery was very slow and painful. The last of these three Dark Ages extinguished Roman civilization in Western Europe in the fifth century A.D. Not until the thirteenth century were equivalent living standards achieved; the recovery thus took eight hundred years.

Society again fell into a Malthusian trap in the fourteenth century. Again recovery was slow, though more sure this time, as intermediate technology spread more widely and methods of handling and employing money became more sophisticated. As late as the first half of the eighteenth century, however, it was rare for even the most advanced economies, those of England and Holland, to achieve 1 per cent growth in any year. And there is a possibility that mankind would again have fallen into a Malthusian trap toward the end of the eighteenth century if industrial capitalism had not made its dramatic appearance.

And it *was* dramatic. By the beginning of the 1780s, in England, an unprecedented annual growth rate of 2 per cent had been achieved. During that decade, the 2 per cent was raised to 4 per cent. This was the great historic "liftoff," and a 4 per cent annual compound growth rate was sustained for the next fifty years. Since this English, and also Scottish, performance was accompanied by the export of capital, patents, machine tools, and skilled manpower to several other advanced nations, the phenomenon soon became international.

A few more figures are necessary to show the magnitude of the change that industrial capitalism brought to human society. In Britain, for instance, in the nineteenth century, the size of the working population multiplied fourfold. Real wages doubled in the half-century 1800-1850, and doubled again, 1850-1900. This meant there was a 1600 per cent increase in the production and consumption of wage-goods during the century. Nothing like this had happened anywhere before, in the whole of history. From the 1850s onward, in Belgium, France, Austria-Hungary, and above all in Germany and the United States, even higher growth rates were obtained; and feudal empires like Japan and Russia were able to telescope into a mere generation or two a development process that in Britain had stretched over centuries.

The growth rates of twelve leading capitalist countries averaged 2.7 per cent a year over the whole fifty-year period up to World War I. There was, it is true, a much more mixed performance between the wars. The United States, which in the forty-four years up to 1914 had averaged a phenomenal 4.3 per cent growth rate, and which in the seven years up to 1929 had increased its national income by a staggering 40 per cent, then saw its national income fall 38 per cent in a mere four years, 1929-32.

But after World War II, growth was resumed on an even more impressive scale. In the 1950s, for instance, the twelve leading capitalist economies cited before had an average annual growth of 4.2 per cent. In Germany it was as high as an average of 7.6 per cent. In all the West European economies, the rate of investment in the 1950s was half again as high as it had ever been on a a sustained basis. In several such countries it was over 20 per cent of the GNP; in Germany and the Netherlands it was 25 per cent, in Norway even higher. Moreover, this high capital formation took place not at the cost of private consumption but during a rapid and sustained rise in living standards, particularly of industrial workers. These tendencies were prolonged throughout the 1960s and into the 1970s. For the mature economies, the second industrial revolution—1945-70—was entirely painless. This was also largely true in Japan, which achieved even higher investment and growth rates in an effort to catch up with the United States and Europe.

In short, after nearly five recorded millennia of floundering about in poverty, humanity suddenly in the 1780s began to hit on the right formula: industrial capitalism. Consider the magnitude of the change over the last two centuries or less. We all know the wealth of present-day West Germany. In the year 1800, in the whole of Germany fewer than 1,000 people had annual incomes as high as $1,000. Or again, take France. France now has more automobiles per capita even than Germany, and more second homes per family than any other country in Europe. In the 1780s, four-fifths of the French families spent 90 per cent of their incomes simply on buying bread—only bread—to stay alive.

In short, industrial capitalism, judged simply by its capacity to create wealth and to distribute it, is a phenomenon unique in world history. One could argue that it is the greatest single blessing ever bestowed on humanity. Why, then, are we asking, "Has capitalism a future?" The answer is clear enough: because capitalism is threatened.

The idea has got around that industrial capitalism is unpopular and always has been, that it is the work of a tiny minority who have thrust it upon the reluctant mass of mankind. Nothing could be further from the truth. The storage economies of remote antiquity were often hideously unpopular. So was the slave-based economy, combined with corporatism, of the classical world. Agricultural feudalism was certainly unpopular, and mercantilism had to be enforced, in practice, by authoritarian states.

But from the very start industrial capitalism won the approval of the masses. They could not vote in the ballot box, but they voted in a far more impressive manner: with their feet. The poorest member of society values political freedom as much as the richest. But the freedom he values most of all is the freedom to sell his labor and skills in the open market, and it was precisely *this* that industrial capitalism gave to men for the first time in history. Hence it is a profound error of fact, in my view, to see what Blake called the "dark, satanic mills" of the industrial revolution as the enslavement of man. The factory system, however harsh it may have been, was the road to freedom for millions of agricultural workers. Not only did it offer them an escape from rural poverty, which was deeper and more degrading than anything experienced in the cities, but it allowed them to move from status to contract, from a stationary place in a static society, with tied cottages and semi-conscript labor, to a mobile place in a dynamic society.

That was why the common man voted for industrial capitalism with his feet, by tramping from the countryside to the towns in enormous numbers, first in Britain, then throughout Europe. And tens of millions of European peasants, decade after decade, moved relentlessly across the Atlantic in pursuit of that same freedom, from semi-feudal estates and small holdings in Russia, Poland, Germany, Austria-Hungary, Italy, Ireland, Scandinavia, to the mines and factories and workshops of New York, Chicago, Pittsburgh, Cleveland, Detroit. It was the first time in history that really large numbers of ordinary people were given the chance to exercise a choice about their livelihood and destiny, and to move, not as members of a tribe or conscript soldiers, but as free individuals, selling their labor in the open market.

They voted for industrial capitalism with their feet not only because they felt in their bones that it meant a modest prosperity for their children and grandchildren—and on the whole they have been proved abundantly right —but because they knew it meant a new degree of freedom for themselves. Indeed, the success of industrialization, despite all its evils, continues to persuade countless ordinary men and women, all over the world, to escape the poverty and restraints of the rural status society and to enter the free labor markets of the towns. Hence the growth of megalopolises all over the world—Calcutta and Bombay, Teheran and Caracas, Mexico City and Djakarta, Shanghai and Lagos, Cairo and Johannesburg. There are now literally scores of million-plus cities all over the Third World. This never-ending one-way flow from countryside to city is plainly a voluntary mass choice, for most governments fear and resent it, and many are attempting, sometimes savagely but always ineffectively, to halt or reverse it. It is more marked in the free-market economies, but it is noticeable everywhere.

Short of evacuating the cities by force and terror, as is now apparently being practiced in parts of southeast Asia, there is no way to stop this human flood. There seems to be an almost irresistible urge in human beings to move away from the status society to contractual individualism, the central feature of industrial capitalism. This operates even in totalitarian societies, as witness the efforts, for instance, of the Chinese and Polish governments to limit the urban explosions they are experiencing.

If industrial capitalism is unique in its wealth-producing capacity and also has the endorsement of the people, then why is it under threat? And who is threatening it?

The Intellectual and Moral Battle

Let me look at five principal elements. The *first,* and in some ways the most important, is that *the free-enterprise idea is losing, if it has not already lost, the intellectual and moral battle.* Not long ago I went into Blackwell's, the great book shop at Oxford University. I wandered over the huge room that houses the books on politics and economics, and having been disagreeably surprised by what I saw there, I made a rough calculation. New books extolling the economic, social, and moral virtues of Communism and collectivism—and there were literally hundreds and hundreds from all over the world—outnumbered books defending free enterprise, or merely seeking to take an objective view of the argument, by between five and six to one. This overwhelming predominance of collectivism was not due to any sinister policy on the part of Blackwell's, which is a highly efficient capitalist enterprise. It was a marketing response to demand on the part of students and teachers. And this was not one of the new slum universities of recent years, some of which have been virtually shanghaied by Marxist factions, but Oxford University, one of the free world's greatest centers of learning, where the battle of ideas is fought under the best possible conditions.

There can be no doubt that the intellectual and moral assault on free enterprise, and the exaltation of Marxist collectivism, that is such a striking feature of the 1970s is directly related to the huge expansion of higher education, put through at such cost to the capitalist economies in the 1960s. Now there is in this a huge and tragic irony. For in the 1950s, the decade when the university expansion was planned, it was the prevailing wisdom among the leading thinkers of the West that the growth of higher education was directly productive of industrial growth—that the more university graduates we turned out, the faster the GNPs of the West would rise. This was the thesis outlined by President Clark Kerr of Berkeley in his 1963 Godkin lectures at Harvard, and it was a thesis put forward in Britain with immense effect by Sir Charles, now Lord Snow. Kerr said: "What the railroads did for the second half of the last century, and the automobile for the first half of this century, may be done for the second half of the twentieth century by the knowledge industry: that is, to serve as the focal point for national growth." He added that more graduates would not only mean a bigger GNP but act as a reinforcement for middle-class democracy, with all its freedoms.

To speak of the "knowledge industry" was to ask for trouble. Knowledge is not a manufactured commodity. There is knowledge for good and knowledge for evil, as the Book of Genesis says. The 1960s, during which most Western nations doubled and some even trebled their university places, did not reinforce democratic freedoms or enlarge the GNP or strengthen the free-enterprise system. They produced the students' revolts, beginning in Paris in 1968. They detonated the Northern Ireland conflict, which is still harassing Britain. They produced the Baader-Meinhoff Gang in West Germany, the Red Brigade in Italy, the Left Fascist terrorism of Japan. They produced an enormous explosion of Marxist studies, centered on the social sciences and especially sociology and on a new generation of school and university teachers who are dedicated, by a sort of perverted religious piety, to the spread of Marxist ideas.

There are ironies within the general irony. The new university of the air, created in Britain at enormous expense to bring higher education to adults and therefore christened the Open University, has become virtually closed to any teacher not of proven Marxist opinions. Nuffield College, Oxford, founded by the great capitalist pioneer Lord Nuffield, who created the British automobile industry, has become a center of trade-union ideology, of the very ideas that slowly but surely are putting the British automobile industry out of world markets and out of business. Warwick University, created in the 1960s as a powerhouse of ideas and clever graduate executives for the West Midlands industrial complex, Britain's biggest, has become a seminary of Marxist and pseudo-Marxist agitators dedicated to the destruction of the wealth-producing machine that brought their university into existence.

I could go on. It is true, of course, that student unrest, as such, has quieted down. But the steady diffusion of ideas hostile to our free system continues remorselessly. Industrial capitalism and the free-market system are presented as destructive of human happiness, corrupt, immoral, wasteful, inefficient, and above all, doomed. Collectivism is presented as the only way out compatible with the dignity of the human spirit and the future of our race. The expanded university threatens to become not the powerhouse of Western individualism and enterprise but its graveyard.

The Ecological Panic

There is a *second* threat, what I have called *the "ecological panic."* This movement, again, began with the best intentions. I well remember when Rachel Carson's book *The Silent Spring* first appeared in the *New Yorker*. The wave of concern that followed was justified. We were tending to ignore some of the destructive side effects of very rapid industrial expansion. The steps then taken, notably the clean-air policies and the policies for cleansing lakes and waterways, have been spectacularly successful. Thanks to smokeless fuel, London fogs, which were real killers, have been virtually eliminated; the last really serious one was in 1952. The Thames is now cleaner and has greater quantities of fish, and more varieties, than at any time since before the days of Spenser or Shakespeare. Similar successes are now being registered in the United States, which adopted such legally enforceable remedies somewhat later than Britain did. These are examples of what can be done by the thoughtful, unemotional, systematic, and scientifically justified application of conservation and anti-pollution policies.

But most of these were put in motion before the ecological panic started. Once ecology became a fashionable good cause, as it did in the late 1960s, reason, logic, and proportion flew out the window. It became a campaign not against pollution but against growth itself, and especially against free-enterprise growth—totalitarian Communist growth was somehow less morally offensive. I highly recommend Professor Wilfred Beckerman's *In Defence of Economic Growth*. Beckerman is one of the best of our economists and was a member of the Royal Commission on Environmental Pollution; he knows the subject better perhaps than any other working economist, and his book is a wonderfully sane and lucid summary of it.

I have never yet been able to persuade any committed ecology campaigner even to look at this book. Of course not. Such persons have a faith, and they do not want to risk it. One of the most important developments of our time is the growth, as a consequence of the rapid decline of Christianity, of irrational substitutes for it. These are not necessarily religious or even quasi-religious. Often they are pseudo-scientific in form, as for instance the weird philosophy of the late Teilhard de Chardin. The ecology panic is another example. It is akin to the salvation panic of sixteenth-century Calvinism. When you expel the priest, you do not inaugurate the age of reason—you get the witch doctor. But whereas Calvinist salvation panic may have contributed to the rise of capitalism, the ecology panic could be the death of it.

If the restrictions now imposed on industrial development had operated in eighteenth-century England, the industrial revolution could not have taken place. It would in effect have been inhibited by law—as of course many landowners of the day wished it to be—and legal requirements would have eliminated the very modest profits by which it originally financed itself. We would still be existing at eighteenth-century living standards, and wallowing in eighteenth-century levels of pollution, which were infinitely worse than anything we experience today. (If you want to see what they were like, visit the slums of Calcutta or Djakarta.)

As it is, the ecology panic has been a potent destructive force. The panic-mongers played a crucial role in persuading the Middle Eastern oil producers, especially Iran, to quadruple the price of oil in the autumn of 1973, the biggest single blow industrial capitalism has suffered since the Wall Street crash of 1929. That was the beginning of the profound recession from which we have not yet emerged. In the end, as was foreseeable at the time, the huge rise in oil prices did not do anyone any good, least of all the oil producers. But it ended the great post-war boom and robbed Western capitalism of its tremendous élan, perhaps for good. As Browning put it,

"Never glad confident morning again." And it is significant that the ecological lobby is now striving with fanatic vigor and persistence to prevent the development of nuclear energy, allegedly on the grounds of safety. Now it is a fact, a very remarkable fact in my view, that throughout the West (we have no figures for Russia or China) the nuclear power industry is the only industry, the *only* industry, which over a period of thirty years has not had a single fatal industrial accident. This unique record has been achieved by the efforts of the industry itself and the responsible governments, without any assistance from the ecolobby. But of course they would *like* a few fatal accidents. That would suit their purposes very well.

In Britain we had a long public enquiry, what we call a statutory enquiry, into whether or not it was right to go ahead with the enriched-uranium plant at Windscale. The enquiry was a model of its kind. The ecolobby marshalled all the scientific experts and evidence they could lay their hands on. At the end the verdict was that there was no reason whatever why the program should not proceed. Did the ecolobby accept the verdict? On the contrary. They immediately organized a mass demonstration and planned various legal and illegal activities to halt the program by force. It is notable that a leading figure in this campaign is the man who is perhaps Britain's leading Communist trade unionist, Mr. Arthur Scargill of the Mine-workers. He has never, so far as we know, campaigned against Soviet nuclear programs, peaceful or otherwise. It is true that most people in the movement in the United States, Britain, France, Germany, and Italy, so far as I have been able to observe, are not politically motivated; they are simply irrational. But irrationality is an enemy of civilized society, and it is being exploited by the politically interested.

Big Government vs. the Market

A *third* factor in the future of capitalism is *the growth of government.* Industrial capitalism—or rather, the free-enterprise economy—and big government are natural and probably irreconcilable enemies. It is no accident that the industrial revolution took place in late eighteenth-century England, a time of minimum government. Of all the periods of English history, indeed of European history, it was the time when government was least conspicuous and active. It was the age, very short alas, of the Night Watchman state. As a matter of fact, the industrial revolution—perhaps the most important single event in human history—seems to have occurred without the English government's even noticing. By the time the government did notice, it was, happily, too late.

It is almost inevitable that government, particularly an active, interventionist government, should view free enterprise with a degree of hostility, since it constitutes a countervailing power in the state. The tendency, then, is to cut free enterprise down to size, in a number of ways. In the United States the characteristic technique is government regulation and legal harassment, and this of course has been far more pervasive and strident since the ecolobby swung into action. In Britain the technique is both direct assault—nationalization—and slow starvation. In a way, nationalization is ineffective, since it allows the public to make comparisons between the performance of the nationalized sector and that of the free sector, nearly always to the latter's advantage.

Starvation is more insidious. By this I mean the progressive transfer of resources, by taxation and other government policies, from the private to the public sector. In 1955, for instance, public expenditure in Britain as a proportion of the GNP was just over 40 per cent. By 1975, twenty years later, it had risen to nearly 60 per cent. This was accompanied by a record budget deficit of about $22 billion, itself a further $11\frac{1}{2}$ per cent of the GNP. Of course, the tax money had to be provided, and the deficit serviced, by the private sector. We have, then, an Old Man of the Sea relationship in which the parasitical Old Man is growing bigger, and poor Sinbad smaller, all the time. The shrinking productive sector has to carry the burden of an ever-expanding loss-making public sector. Thus Britain's authorized steel industry will lose $1 billion this year, and it has been authorized by statute to borrow up to $7 billion, guaranteed by government and taxpayer. Now the interesting thing is that in Britain the public sector and the civil service generally are now paying higher wages, providing better conditions, and giving larger pensions—which in a growing number of cases are index-linked and thus inflation-proof—than the private sector can possibly afford. And of course they are financing these goodies out of tax-guaranteed deficits—that is, from the dwindling profits of the private sector. This is what I call the starvation technique. When a private firm goes bust, provided it is big enough, the state takes over, the losses are added to the taxpayer's bill, and the private sector has one more expensive passenger to carry.

In this technique, the *fourth* factor, *the trade unions,* play an important part. In Britain it is demonstrably true that the legal privileges of the trade unions, which virtually exempt them from any kind of action for damages (including, now, libel), led directly to restrictive practices, over-manning, low productivity, low investment, low wages, and low profits. Thus trade-union action tends, in itself, to undermine the performance of industrial capitalism as a wealth-creating system. In Britain, the trade unions can rightly claim that capitalism is inefficient, because they make sure it is inefficient. Ford workers in Britain, using exactly the same assembly-line machinery as in West Germany, produce between 20 per cent and 50 per cent fewer automobiles. ICI Chemicals, one of the best companies in Britain, nevertheless has a productivity performance 25 per cent lower than its Dutch and German competitors. A recent analysis shows this is entirely due to over-manning and restrictive practices.

The private sector in Britain is now threatened by two further union devices: the legally enforced closed shop, which compels workers to join designated unions on pain of dismissal without compensation or legal redress, and new plans to force firms to have up to 50 per cent worker directors, appointed not by the work force themselves nor even necessarily from among them but by and from the trade-union bureaucracy (Bullock Report). This has to be seen against the explicit policy of some groups within the unions of driving private-sector firms to bankruptcy by strikes and harassment, so that the state will then have to take them into the public sector.

What is happening in Britain will not necessarily happen elsewhere. But there are many ways in which the present U.S. administration seems determined to follow Britain's example. The West Germans, too, are now beginning to adopt some of the institutions that flourish in British trade unionism, notably the shop stewards' movement. Businessmen all over the free world may despise the performance of British industry, but trade unionists all over the world admire and envy the power of British trade unionists and are actively seeking to acquire it for themselves.

The Totalitarian Threat

Let me end on a word of warning. I have said nothing of the *fifth* threat to industrial capitalism and the free-enterprise system—*the threat from without*. But this is bound to increase as the military superiority of the Soviet Union over the United States is reinforced. I have never thought that the Communist system would triumph by a direct assault. I have always assumed that it would first establish an overwhelming military predominance and then, by pressure and threats, begin to draw the political and economic dividends of it. If the United States opts out of the competitive arms race with the Soviet Union while supposedly providing merely for its own defense, then we must expect to see this fifth threat hard at work winding up industrial capitalism and free enterprise all over the world.

Therefore, when we ask, "Has capitalism a future?," I answer: It all depends on the United States. West Germany and Japan, it is true, have strong free-enterprise economies; they also have a tradition of state capitalism, and would adapt themselves with surprising speed and readiness to a new collective order. France already has a huge public sector and a long tradition of *dirigisme* or *étatisme*. All three are Janus-faced. Britain, I believe, is profoundly anti-collective and will remain so if it continues to be given the choice. But its private-enterprise system is now very weak, and its business and financial elites are demoralized and defeatist.

I myself think that capitalism will survive, because of its enormous intrinsic virtues as a system for generating wealth and promoting freedom. But those who man and control it must stop apologizing and go on the ideological offensive. They must show ordinary people that both the Communist world and the Third World are parasitical upon industrial capitalism for their growth technology, and that without capitalism, the 200 years of unprecedented growth that have created the modern world would gradually come to an end. We would have slow growth, then nil growth, then minus growth, and then the Malthusian catastrophe.

Those who wish to maintain the capitalist system must endeavor to teach the world a little history. They must remind it, and especially the young, that though man's achievements are great, they are never as solid as they look. If man makes the wrong choice, there is always another Dark Age waiting for him round the corner of time.

THE RESPONSES

HERBERT SCHMERTZ

1. Democracy, Tyranny, and Capitalism

WHILE I AM ALL FOR capitalism and see many valid points in Paul Johnson's argument, I get uneasy when I see it posed—as I think Johnson does—as the antithesis to Marxism or "Marxist collectivism." Marxism is at best a theory about history and at worst what the economist P. T. Bauer has called "an all-embracing secular messianic faith." Capitalism is neither. It is a historical phenomenon, as Johnson points out, but even by his own definition it is an economic system: a device, a means, a way to go about certain economic business. It is hardly a theory about history, and much less is it the force that must be set in the lists to combat the messianic faith of Marxist collectivism. I would guess that the faith of capitalists is invested in far more profound and transcendent realities than capitalism. What they see and fear in Marxist collectivism is not so much its menace to capitalism as its menace to freedom.

This distinction is important. There is some danger that readers of Johnson's essay may come away believing that the struggle is between capitalism and Marxism. That is to wage the battle on Marxism's ground and in Marxism's terms, and it renders the contest deceptively simple. Marxism's argument is only superficially with capitalism: witness the cordiality of Marxist states when they are in need of high technology. At its essence, Marxism's

HERBERT SCHMERTZ *is a director and vice-president for public affairs of the* Mobil Corporation. *His portfolio includes public relations, domestic and international government relations, and urban affairs.*

argument is about who shall make choices; it is a quarrel with freedom and democracy.

Given this perspective, I am somewhat hesitant about the broad scope of Johnson's thesis. That the industrial revolution was an epochal event must be admitted, but Europe was by no means sick and poor when the industrial revolution began. Revolutionary economic changes had been initiated in the sixteenth century with the voyages of discovery and the considerable stimulation of trade, industry, and finance provoked by these discoveries. And—at least on this side of the ocean—we tend to assign even more importance to the revolution of ideas that might be said to have begun with the Magna Carta, developed in the Enlightenment, and culminated in the American Revolution: the idea that governments must answer to the people.

From such a perspective, the threats to capitalism outlined by Johnson seem less formidable. We have seen that the university student's infatuation with collectivism tends to fade rather quickly once he begins to work within the capitalistic system and learns to recognize its virtues. We have seen, in the United States at least, a growing public realization that balance is necessary in questions that pit environmentalism against the need for energy, economic growth, and jobs; people are becoming more enlightened about the tradeoffs required in a progressive society. Americans have already begun a more careful definition of the role to be played by government in relation to enterprise and the market economy, as evidenced by the deregulation of airline fares and the movement toward decontrol of prices for natural gas and crude oil.

These are arguments that capitalism has begun to win on the basis of facts and experience—on pragmatic, economic grounds. I would say that it is all very well to go on the "ideological offensive" but that one must be careful not to confuse ideology and economics, lest—as in Marxism—the one poison the other.

Many writers and scholars present capitalism as a scheme of social organization, a remarkable fortress of ideology and philosophy concerning the right to private property, strict limitation of government power, and dedication to free markets or the market economy. Yet capitalism itself has displayed, in the main, a positive aversion to ideology, to declaring itself the one true way that men should live and work. Its claims—and demonstrated virtues—have mainly to do with the economic sphere. This is why multinational corporations are able to operate successfully and usefully in so many countries, with so many ideological shadings in their governments. For they enable economics to stand apart from politics.

Still, I suppose we are observing the phenomenon Bertolt Brecht described when he said that to avoid ideology in our day is not to escape it. Presenting capitalism as a scheme of social organization gives the scholar a convenient rhetorical device to oppose to socialism or "Marxist collectivism." He can then argue private property vs. public ownership, market economy vs. centrally controlled economy, or limited government vs. all-pervasive government.

But the scheme of social organization in, say, the United States is not capitalism but democracy. Americans, if asked, do not describe themselves as capitalists. Capitalism, to the man in the street, is not the ideological fortress underlying his liberties but an economic system that has worked rather well (as Johnson points out) for almost every group or individual who got involved with it. As long as we talk about capitalism in terms of what it is—an economic device of proven value—it can generally hold its own in the public dialogue. But we shall send people scurrying off in droves if we attempt to load the nature and fate of Western civilization onto the back of capitalism. I think Americans know very well that what Marxism can imperil is their liberty, not their capitalism.

It is worth remembering that to offer a convincing catalogue of the dangers or abject failures of socialism does not, in itself, convert one's listeners to capitalism. This seems to have mystified a fair number of capitalist intellectuals; it is perhaps further evidence of the perils encountered when ideology and economics are confused.

Can we look at capitalism without its ideological freight? Perhaps by thinking of it as simply a "competitive market economy" we can consider it as an economic system. As Johnson describes most forcefully, capitalism has worked phenomenally well in achieving material abundance, the wide distribution of goods, and a steady increase in personal opportunity. I think we can discern in the system of capitalism some sort of inner affinity with the human desire to work, to make or build or accomplish something of one's own, and an even deeper affinity with the human desire to change, to improve not only one's self but also one's environment. Capitalism has not created these needs; it has merely provided a marvelous means for fulfilling them. When critics complain that capitalism has aggravated spiritual unease or restlessness in Western civilization, they overlook the possibility that this very restlessness has perhaps created and formed the civilization.

Capitalism has been not a primary cause but an efficient vehicle.

Johnson's warning that capitalism can be smothered, dismantled, and destroyed is valid. I think there is some danger that this will happen in the United States, but I am, on the whole, optimistic that it will not. Even in the worst of times, many of us have persisted in believing that the American public—given more information—would come to see that the market prospers in liberty and atrophies under command.

That lesson of history is so clear that it cannot forever be ignored. It is an idea that is currently in disfavor among many American intellectuals. But the public is of a different mind. The public current is now running strongly against big government and excessive, costly regulation—witness California's Proposition 13 and similar tax revolts. The public demand is for change, for a thorough pruning of the huge, remote bureaucracies that have been interfering so relentlessly not only with the free market but with almost everyone's life and work.

And even the intellectual community is beginning to resist the unnecessary interference of government in what had been an effective and highly successful market economy. In 1978 the new president of Yale University, A. Bartlett Giamatti, went to some length in his inaugural address to remind the Yale community of the dangers to Yale of "governmental intrusion" and to stress that private educational institutions "are an integral part of the private sector." He called for an end to the "ancient ballet of mutual antagonism" between private enterprise and private education, and said further: "There is a metaphor that informs the private business sector as it informs the private educational sector, and that is the metaphor of the free marketplace."

And of course there are other striking signs of the change in public opinion. Legislators themselves are becoming disenchanted with the unpredictable distortions and misallocations of resources that result from large-scale government interference in the operations of the market economy. They are coming to see the truth in Friedrich Hayek's observation that the competitive free market does not mean a national abdication from planning; rather, "competition means decentralized planning by many separate persons."

Inherent in the competitive market economy, in capitalism, there *is* a plan—a sort of unorchestrated harmony that represents not only the decisions of "many separate persons" but also the larger frame of public decisions and reasonable regulations that channel enterprise toward goals aligned with the democratic ideal. This is not true *laissez-faire* capitalism—if indeed there has ever been such a creature outside books—but rather a system in which the public sector takes pains to foster responsive, adaptable, innovative, and democratic markets. That system worked in an extraordinary, unprecedented way to advance the material well-being and range for personal autonomy of all those who took part in it. Today the public, much of the intellectual community, and many of the nation's political leaders show a growing appreciation of that system's worth—heartening evidence that capitalism does indeed have a future.

PAUL SEABURY

2. The Exquisitely Sensitive Market

A FEW YEARS AGO IN BRITAIN I read a column in the Paris *Herald Tribune* by Anthony Lewis, who was then living in London. According to Lewis, a poll of its readers made by the English journal *New Society* confirmed his belief that English life was preferable to American. A substantial majority of that journal's subscribers—who are largely sociologists and social workers—asserted that they actually preferred to receive their real income in the form of social services, welfare benefits, and the like, rather than in cash. This inspired Lewis to expatiate on the vulgarity of his money-grubbing American countrymen, out for a quick buck and made miserable by the demeaning activity of the work this goal entailed.

(A few days later I was in that London gourmet palace called Fortnum and Mason's when what to my wondering eyes did appear but the same Mr. Lewis, in a natty Edwardian costume, at the wine counter. Curiosity drew me to this scene of an actual cash transaction as Mr. Lewis, in need of one of the best years of Chateau Lafite-Rothschild, sent an aged retainer scrambling up and down the cellar staircase bringing up bottles that he then inspected with impeccable hauteur. But I digress.)

I have no idea what the results of such a poll might have been had its sample been more representative of the English public at large, but it is

---

PAUL SEABURY *is a professor of political science at the University of California, Berkeley. He has written numerous books on foreign policy and articles on a wide range of public issues.*

hardly surprising that social workers and sociologists hold such views. In England and in America also, many people are quite taken with the vision of a way of life that can be both dependable and dependent. This has considerable bearing upon the puzzle that Paul Johnson sets before us: Why is there so much resentment against an economic system that has brought so much real wealth to such vast numbers of people?

I suspect that when you come down to it, most people in so-called capitalist societies are of two minds about the ground rules of pure capitalism. Medieval and socialist societies, in both their real and their ideal forms, and however impoverished, offer regularities that capitalism in its purer forms cannot. This is no novel insight, but it needs to be noted.

The market system, with its laws of supply and demand, is exquisitely sensitive to changes in what people want and what people are willing to part with or to produce. The modern corporation seems best suited to do this on a large scale. Capitalism also is remarkably tolerant of what people wish to make of their lives as producers, workers, and consumers. It appeals to the ambitious, creative, and calculating sides of our nature. The classic Yankee took to it like a fish to water. When latent energies are released, a spurt of growth and innovation will occur. The main technological advances of the nineteenth century resulted from the efforts of countless thousands of innovators—tinkerers, scientists, mechanics—in whom a creative curiosity was coupled with a strong work ethic and a zeal for becoming better off.

But the logic of medievalism and socialism and the logic of capitalism appeal to contrary aspects of our nature. I am now referring not to socialism as a revolutionary movement out to overthrow the ruling class but rather to socialism as an established way of life, as manifested variously both in Western welfare democracies and in cruel totalitarian countries. Socialism offers surcease from some of the uncertainties of a capitalistic world. The medieval system offered the certainty of a heritable status whose constraints on human potential precluded the anxieties that attend the exercise of choice and free movement. Modern socialism does not offer a reality of plenty (the reality is more often that of rationing, shortages, and queues); it offers security within strict official rules.

Socialism, moreover, is more easily at home with communalism than is capitalism. At its best, the latter is a "community of competitors and strivers," defined without regard to race, color, nationality, or religion. Socialism is typically suspicious of any form of cosmopolitanism, which subverts close and tribal structures. The truly popular socialisms of our time, such as National Socialism, reject market principles since these subvert tribal values. Castro's cane-cutting battalions, whacking their way through the plantations, are meant to be manifestations of militant solidarity as much as or more than economic activity.

Under socialism, people are officially cared for and are expected to reciprocate by meeting prescribed norms. Everything is theirs and nothing is theirs. Caring-for is both a form of teaching and a form of regulating. It may often be justified as a way of lessening the risks and uncertainties of everyday life. Also, it is a morally impeccable occupation, justified on the grounds either of public safety or of protection. There can be no particular objection to it until it becomes a governing preoccupation of a political system, or an obsession of those for whom risk-diminution is the way in which life is perceived. (I recently noticed on the Stanford University campus a carpenter carrying an ordinary ladder that had a label on it: OSHA approved. A federal inspector had inspected a qualified carpenter's ladder and found it safe! The carpenter struck me as a man able to tell a lark from a ladder; when I asked him how often the inspector came around to look at it, he was not amused.)

Today anyone who publicly comes out against too much official caring for us risks being regarded as either inhumane, irresponsible, or unrealistic. Yet the problem remains: when risk-elimination becomes the governing preoccupation of reformers and managers, prudence—an ordinary virtue—gives way to stultification.

Today this concern for regulated safety permeates American life; we are thought to require every precaution from 100 per cent safe nuclear installations to plastic toys that infants cannot eat and aspirin bottles that able-bodied adults can scarcely open. (It is an odd contradiction that as government regulation spreads through our society, that society continues to be in other respects increasingly permissive.) The penalties of overregulation are obvious. For one, a whole region of North America—New England—risks falling into industrial desuetude simply in order to avoid risk to clams and louseworts and the hazards of hypothetical oil spills and nuclear accidents. It is important to notice that these crusades are not initiated chiefly by governments (federal or state); often they are pushed upon governments by articulate interest groups. Democracy works!

Turning now to Paul Johnson's thesis, while I find considerable truth in it, I also detect an exaggeration so considerable that it defeats the commendable purposes he has in mind. If the five factors he names are indeed threats to modern capitalism, then together they appear overwhelming: universities (and university students), ecologists, government, trade unions, and our obstinate Soviet adversary. Yet I am sure Johnson would agree that the first four of them have made *some* contribution to the sustenance and quality of the American economy.

To take only one of the four, the trade unions: while the British experience sharply differs from the American, it should be pointed out that American labor has stoutly supported the free-enterprise system and has resisted the lures of both socialization and nationalization. Moreover, through the AFL-CIO it today plays a major role in drawing the American public's attention to the awesome challenge of Soviet military and strategic power. Furthermore, since jobs are often the first victims of ecological crusades, labor does not ignore threats of ecological injunctions. I recall a moving event recently in San Francisco: when lawyers representing the Sierra Club and Friends of the Earth obtained a court order stopping the construction of an additional parking facility at the San Francisco airport, the head of the construction workers' union declared at a press conference: "The Friends of the Earth are not the friends of man!" (He spoke these words in company with the president of the Chamber of Commerce.) In such weighty matters, it would seem that those who are concerned with the quality and performance of a free economy should seek out coalitions based upon clear common interests.

However—and here I turn to a point that Johnson neglects—capitalism itself is not wholly free from the suspicion that its dynamics are not always at work on behalf of free societies. The spectacle of American business firms and banks rushing in to develop the infrastructure of the Soviet industrial system as a way of making money is but one example (commercial pornography is another) of how the profit motive is not always congruent with the interests of a free society.

A more sensible approach to the problem of modern capitalism in our complex world would be one that judges it, as well as its rivals and companions, according to public-interest criteria that are not exclusively derived from the inner logic of any one of them. Right now, Johnson's diagnosis of the current situation has some ominous truth in it, for the spreading web of regulatory constraints upon capitalism in the interests of safety, security, "purity," and social justice exacts a heavy toll on the economy and the public. The specter of a runaway process whereby essentially unproductive or counterproductive movements overwhelm the productive ones in our culture is disquieting to behold. It is excesses, including the excesses of purist zealots, that have given government, the ecological movement, the universities, and unions a bad name. Yet each of these institutions has an intrinsic virtue that should not be overlooked.

The "Friends of Capitalism" should have the common sense to recognize and exploit sensible coalitions. Persons who are well disposed toward one or another of the elements that Johnson sees as internal threats to capitalism could see ways in which common cause with business can be mutually beneficial. Labor, for instance, has not been as alert as it should be to the depredations of ecological zealotry. Universities have been too supine in accepting federal regulatory controls of their activities. And ecologists should be warned that the purest "ecology" would be one in which even Sierra Clubbers were forbidden to poach on Nature's divine terrain.

ALAN REYNOLDS

3. Maximizing Free Choice

PAUL JOHNSON HAS REDISCOVERED the central role of economic freedom, both as an end in itself and as a means of social advancement through individual achievement. He warns that prolonged periods of economic contraction have occurred before and could again. In particular, we cannot safely assume continued progress of the sort that we have experienced under a non-system (imperfectly described as "industrial capitalism") that maximizes individual choice.

Johnson lists several perceived threats to a reasonably free and productive economy. We are told, for example, that the free-enterprise idea is losing "the intellectual and moral battle," and we are offered as evidence the fact that in one British bookstore collectivist books outnumber those defending free enterprise. We are also reminded of the student unrest of a decade ago.

Johnson has been visiting the wrong bookstore in the wrong country. In the United States, if collectivist literature is not outnumbered, it is certainly outclassed. Dozens of think tanks, economics departments, and journals with a distinctly favorable attitude toward capitalism have sprung up during the past decade. The Keynesian nostrums, regulatory rampage, and egalitarian sentimentalism of the 1960s are now clearly on the defensive in

ALAN REYNOLDS *is a vice-president and economist with the First National Bank of Chicago. He previously was the economics editor of "National Review" and has published articles on economic policy in various journals.*

intellectual combat—indeed, they are up against the ropes. Students are rushing into solid courses in business and economics and are not wasting time reading Fanon or Marcuse. It may not be so in Britain, but Britain's role today is reduced to serving as a bad example (though we do not know what Margaret Thatcher may accomplish).

Capitalism's tremendous engine of progress is nonetheless quite fragile, in Johnson's view, since the OPEC oil price hike has "robbed Western capitalism of its tremendous élan, perhaps for good." But a free-market economy is a method of handling scarcity, from whatever source, and can hardly be threatened by its primary function.

If we accept the orthodox (but flimsy) forecast that "the age of cheap energy is gone forever," then the shape of production and consumption will have to adapt in order to make use of relatively more abundant resources. Uncontrolled markets are ideally suited to handling such variations in scarcity, and in fact do so without fuss or bother every minute of every day. Market incentives divert scarce resources toward uses that consumers value most highly, while also encouraging suppliers to devise new ways of producing and economizing on the use of those resources. The alternative "system" is usually primitive rationing, through waiting lines, or allocation according to the preferences of politicians and bureaucrats.

Ecological mysticism, says Johnson, threatens to obstruct progress because humanity has a finite capacity for logic and evidence: "When you expel the priest . . . you get the witch doctor." But though environmental extremism is indeed a significant obstacle, the resulting sacrifice of other values is sufficiently apparent to generate a backlash that usually limits the damage. The elitist form of the crusade—preserving scenery or exotic toadstools at the expense of energy, housing, and jobs—is already in retreat.

Britain's "business and financial elites," says Johnson, "are demoralized and defeatist." But why should we expect salvation at the hands of business and financial elites? No businessman worth his perks feels any fondness for competition, or any revulsion toward subsidies and protection. There is nothing deplorable about this. Producers naturally favor scarcity and high prices, and a British-style system that caters to producer interests is a system of institutionalized deprivation.

A free economy should be a consumer movement; it can find its strongest allies among consumers and taxpayers. A free economy, after all, produces a free lunch (consumer surplus) by driving costs and prices below what many would be willing to pay. It compels producers to produce the most of what consumers want with the least use of valued resources; otherwise the producers will not survive in the competition for capital.

Finally, we get closer to the real threat to capitalism and economic growth. Free enterprise and big government are said to be irreconcilable enemies. Big government regulates the private economy into oblivion, says Johnson, or starves it by subsidizing inefficient firms at the expense of the productive. This parasitic syndrome is real enough, though ultimately suicidal even for those lusting after political power. Big government needs a strong economy to finance its often foolish activities. But any method of financing government—levying taxes, borrowing from the private sector, or printing money—can reach destructive proportions. Tax rates can become so steep as to encourage wholesale tax evasion; public borrowing can displace productive uses of private credit; and the printing of money can reach a point where money is treated like a hot potato, producing virulent inflation.

Johnson describes but does not explain the danger of economic decline. So we are left to guard against something formless and indefinite. The threat is surely not his "Malthusian trap," wherein slow growth produces more people than food. Even if slow economic growth were always associated with rapid population growth (Britain's soaring population during the industrial revolution is one of many obvious exceptions), we would still need a systematic explanation of the cause of slow growth. Such an explanation is not hard to construct.

People seem to prefer more to less. And the only legal ways of acquiring more and better goods and services are to produce and trade more or to manipulate the political process to acquire what others produce. These two forces of growth and redistribution are in constant conflict, because it is difficult to keep people producing and investing at full potential when a lot of added work brings only a little more after-tax income. The stick of potential deprivation is a partial substitute for the carrot of reward in the Soviet Union but not in the Western welfare states, where failure or refusal to produce for markets brings transfer payments from those who do produce. Having thrown away the stick, we cannot afford to lose the carrot.

The real threat to capitalism is not that the system lacks intellectual or business support, nor that it cannot adapt to energy and environmental difficulties, nor that it is threatened by some spontaneous burst of overpopulation. The threat is more simple. In order to make good on an accumulation of past political promises, governments must extract an increasingly large share of the production of private labor and capital. If the resources are extracted in a way that penalizes increases in production, production does not increase. The rising tax burden must then fall lower and lower on the income scale.

From this internal contradiction of the welfare state, we come at last to the self-correcting mechanism that restores equilibrium between the forces of growth and redistribution: tax revolt. If Johnson had focused his attention forward to the tax revolt of the coming decade instead of backward to such things as the student revolt of the past decade, he would have discovered the vehicle by which the United States will lead the world back to capitalism.

MICHAEL NOVAK

4. Productivity and Social Justice

PAUL JOHNSON HAS OPENED an important path. For years, intellectuals of the free world have been able to take for granted the prosperity and liberty provided by their economic system. And many have heaped upon that system every sort of moral reproach and rhetorical abuse in the cheapest and most uncritical way possible. More than those in any previous era, intellectuals in the free world today have been given both liberty and ample means of support. Their numbers have swollen enormously. They preside over vast and powerful institutions of culture, not only in the universities and the press but in many other enterprises as well. Along with the rest of their society, they live longer—on the average, thirty years longer than most males or females in human history. They live better. They have books and copying machines, night lights and electric typewriters, computers and huge free libraries. Yet many of these intellectuals loathe their economic system—capitalism—as they loathe no other.

Consider the following typical sentences in a respectable theological publication, *The Ecumenist*:

> One may, of course, argue that no adequate theodicy can possibly be developed in the context of organized capitalistic society, the ability of

MICHAEL NOVAK *is a scholar-in-residence at the American Enterprise Institute and a syndicated columnist. He is the author of "The American Vision: An Essay on the Future of Democratic Capitalism" and other books on politics and religion, as well as two novels.*

which to cause suffering and death—colonialism, imperialism, two world wars, slums, profitable production of carcinogenic food, economic depressions, fascism, Dachau, Hiroshima and Vietnam—is so out of proportion to its capacity truly to heal. . . . For us others, who are not caught in such naiveté, this theodicy remains stuck in our throats in the face of the innocent victims of history, e.g., the victims of the five chronic and terminal culture diseases, one of which, cancer, with its two hundred different forms, is killing thirty percent of the population of advanced capitalistic societies. . . . "You cannot put us into hell," say the men of Brecht's *City of Mahagonny,* symbol of capitalist society, to God, who approaches them at dawn in order to judge them. "You cannot put us into hell, since we have always been in hell!" [Rudolf J. Siebert, "Hans Küng: Toward a Negative Theology?," *The Ecumenist,* January-February, 1979].

(No one knows what hell is who hasn't been brought up in Scarsdale.) Leave aside the fact that the Bertolt Brecht of *The Rise and Fall of the City of Mahagonny* (1930) had not yet seen the hell of Buchenwald and Dachau, and that a tiny band of democratic capitalist nations rose up in mortal combat to throw off the terror of National Socialism. Leave aside the fact that before cancer proved its capacity (whatever it is, from whatever source) to kill so large a proportion of the population, bourgeois standards of health care were required to reduce other killers that for centuries had struck down a majority of the population far earlier in life. (The average life span before capitalism was approximately thirty-seven years.) Leave aside the author's silly reflections on the superior theodicy of secular intellect. Note simply his characterization of democratic capitalism: is it not, in the strictest sense, mad? Except that it is conventional.

Cheap grace, this supposed moral superiority to democratic capitalism. Its theological critics do not nowadays tell us what more liberating system they have recently invented. An exception is the Methodist Federation for Social Action, in Staten Island, New York, which in a study of "capitalism and Christian faith" does tell us:

In keeping with the Federation commitment to replace the present struggle-for-profit system with a just and humane one, and in keeping with the biblical hope for a new creation, the study points toward the possibility for fundamental change in American social, economic, and political institutions. . . . Our hopes move in the direction of socialism . . . a socialism not defined by what exists elsewhere under this name so much as by the particular possibilities of the American situation ["A Critical Study of Capitalism and the Christian Faith"].

Max Weber once wrote that the spirit of capitalism could not have arisen when and how it did without the impulse of Christianity, particularly of Calvinist Christianity. But he could find no Calvinist theologians to cite in support of his thesis (he depended a great deal on Benjamin Franklin's *Autobiography*). It has always been an embarrassment to his thesis that the most Calvinist sections of the world he described—namely, Scotland and Calvin's own Geneva—were at first among the most resistant to the capitalist spirit. Indeed, the major theologians even of the present are virtually unanimous in declaring themselves socialist. In 1933, in *Christ the Center,* Dietrich Bonhoeffer described "the working class world" in which "Jesus can be present on the factory floor as the socialist, in politics as the idealist, in the worker's own world as the good man. He fights in their ranks against the enemy, capitalism." Karl Barth was a socialist, as was Paul Tillich; in his earlier years, Reinhold Niebuhr was a candidate for Congress in the Socialist party. In his Holland lectures for 1949, V. A. Demant summed up the conventional vision in the aphorism: "Christianity is the teaching of which socialism is the practice."

Today the situation demands more exact inquiry. More than eighty nations of the world have now declared themselves socialist republics. Socialism is no longer merely a dream expressed in books. Armies march in its name. Its radical principles and its concrete programs have been tried in many different circumstances. Does socialism diminish alienation? Does it increase liberty? Does it produce wealth and distribute it as efficiently and as broadly as democratic capitalism? Is the gap between the privileged and the many smaller under socialism? Has the nationalization of industries produced its predicted effects? Is state ownership less corrupt than private? Perhaps in self-mockery, Arthur C. Cochrane wrote in *Christianity and Crisis* (April 16, 1979) that "among eighteen non-Communist countries the United States falls behind in the socialization of postal services, telecommunications, electricity, gas, oil, coal, railways, airlines, motor industry, steel and shipbuilding. In fact only the postal service is completely socialized." The post office is his utopia. Empirical intelligence should have a sharper edge.

Inquirers are free to compare the working of socialism with the working of democratic capitalism, and to measure which system produces greater benefits for the poor, greater equality, and greater liberty. On this ground, the question lies open to empirical description. (Intellectuals *are* able to see the facts: they stream out of a more socialist Britain into a less socialist United States.) As Leszek Kolakowski has written in *Marxism,* however, those drawn to socialism are not moved by empirical evidence. Something else moves them, and Kolakowski thinks it is a secular religious passion. The intellectual groundwork for this passion was laid in the humanities and the liberal arts, disciplines earlier given high status under aristocratic regimes. Humanists have long shown a fine aristocratic resentment of the new business class, of the industrial arts and the commercial arts, of the bourgeois ethic and the bourgeois aesthetic. The groundwork was also laid by the rise of the social sciences, particularly sociology, whose fundamental conceptions are implicitly socialist: that society is like a machine, to be quantitatively analyzed and managed by experts (social scientists and simultaneously socialists, scornful of free individuals and free markets).

Theologians, otherwise so skillful in adapting to modernity, are traditionalists about economics (whose study until recently they have ignored). When they write about "social justice," they exhibit two forms of traditionalism. First, they compare modern alienation to a remembered spirit of community and togetherness, as when simple peasants labored for their noble *paterfamilias*. Thus Karl Barth writes that the basic evil in capitalism is that it permits in practice and demands in principle that "man should make another man and his work a means to his own ends, and therefore a mere instrument, and that this is inhuman, and therefore constitutes an injustice." Is Barth's description accurate? No system before democratic capitalism so well defined, enlarged, and institutionalized the rights of individual men and women as ends and not means. A free economy both generates and has as its precondition a free polity. Is Barth's point merely about productive labor? When one of Barth's books was set in type by a printer, was that man merely a means? There is a subordination of means and ends in every human activity; excellence in the work of any one of us (our end, dignifying our labor) is for someone else a means (even a reader uses an author as, in part, a means). This is as true under feudalism, mercantilism, or socialism as under capitalism.

Secondly, theologians are traditionalist when they imagine that the primary problem of social justice is *distribution*. In the static economies of the traditional era, wealth was regarded as fixed and limited. Indeed, until the nineteenth century and the rise of capitalism, the caricature of the quintessentially evil man was the miser. The miser was evil because he hoarded a larger portion of his society's fixed and limited wealth than he could use. His hoarding was someone else's deprivation. The imagination of democratic capitalism broke with traditional economics and traditional ethics on this very point: it made the miser seem absurd, a fool. For wealth can be productive. It can grow. The main problem of social justice is not distribution; it is *production*. Adam Smith changed the canons of traditional ethics when in *The Wealth of Nations* (1776) he pictured the dynamic economic possibilities that lay before not merely individuals but all humankind. He pointed to the ethic of productivity.

Democratic capitalism cannot be judged satisfactorily by the traditional ethics of social justice unless the moralist introduces the dimension of the production of new wealth. It is in this dimension that capitalism has been uniquely beneficial to all nations that have felt its touch. All, without exception, are richer now than before—not only in per capita income and standard of living but also in health, longevity, and the liberties of daily life. The ethic of production precedes the ethic of distribution.

The best of the theologians sound, in economic matters, like the better minds of the fourteenth century. This is particularly sad since economic analysis is more and more the subject of pronouncements by international church bodies. Sooner or later, theologians will have to develop a taste for the secular discipline of economics. They will need to make some empirical comparisons. They will also need some new theological theory to match economic realities.

The working of socialism, for one thing, now lies open to inspection. For too long, the *ideals* of socialism (benignly interpreted) were contrasted with the *practice* of capitalism. As Ottavio Paz has said:

> If there is one profoundly reactionary sector in Latin America, it is the leftist intellectuals. They are people without memory. I have never heard one of them admit he made a mistake. Marxism has become an intellectual vice. It is the superstition of the twentieth century. . . . Look at Cuba. A revolution can be gauged by its ability to transform an economy. Under Batista, Cuba was a monoculture of sugar. Under Castro, Cuba is still a monoculture of sugar. Cuba has changed its dependence, but not its economy. It was sort of an American brothel and now it is a Soviet barracks, a bureaucratic colony [Alan Riding, "For Ottavio Paz, A Solitude of His Own as a Political Rebel," *New York Times,* May 3, 1979].

Theologians ought to study the empirical record of socialism and compare it point by point with that of democratic capitalism. They will find that little is left of the original socialist programs. Socialist practice does not turn out as socialist theory predicts. This is almost certainly because the theory contains the seeds of practical contradiction.

The *ideals* of democratic capitalism also need to be stated. No theologian has ever attempted to do this. Democratic capitalism has three parts: an economic system (market), a political system (democratic), and a cultural system (liberal, pluralistic, often but not always Judeo-Christian). The economists have analyzed the economic system reasonably well, the political scientists the democratic system; but the humanists—not least the theologians—have been colossally deficient in comprehending the relation of our culture's system of symbols, practices, and values to the political system and the economic system. Each of these systems depends upon the other two.

One can foresee some of the directions in which a theological analysis of the ideals of democratic capitalism will have to go. First, the aim of such a social system is the well-being of all mankind, the increased wealth of all nations. This is a humble aim, materialistic in a superficial sense, but in no sense materialistic in its ultimate purpose. For the aim is to liberate humankind by transforming the material base of daily life—to bestow on all a degree of leisure, upward mobility, and opportunity open in previous eras only to a very few.

Second, democratic capitalism is a highly fraternal system, not in the traditional sense of community, but in the sort of associative, cooperative organization of society on which it totally depends. It requires associations of many kinds, and a very enlarged sense of sociality.

Third, democratic capitalism depends upon an accurate reading of human sinfulness, not in order to repress it, and certainly not in order to intensify it, but, rather, in order to bend it to the social benefit of all and to transform it into something creative and liberating. The social purpose of democratic capitalism cannot be said to be, as R. H. Tawney pointed out, mere acquisitiveness. The mere miser is, in a democratic capitalist society, a pathetic figure. Those with capital are placed under moral obligation and systemic pressure. Democratic capitalism rests on the motto "In God we trust"—meaning, in nobody else. In the political, economic, and cultural systems it institutionalizes checks and balances, pluralism, and open competition. It never does so perfectly. But it has a profound self-correcting mechanism built into it so that it is a more change-producing, dynamic, and progressive system than any known before. This mechanism is based upon a sense of sin.

No other economic system has ever been so favorable to the very poor, to so many of whom it has given unprecedented mobility and opportunity.

No other system has so quickly and universally raised the levels of health, longevity, and income of the entire world; even the socialist world lives by its inventions and techniques. None has ever given theologians (among others) so great a liberty or so many perquisites. No other system has ever permitted its critics such ample scope, or drawn so many voluntary migrants from other lands, or bent itself, upon facing its tremendous inadequacies, toward self-improvement. It is not the kingdom of God, and perhaps better systems may be imagined. Indeed, it is the ideal of this system to seek to become better—morally better—and to devise new institutions whereby that happy goal might be accomplished.

Democratic capitalism is by no means an ideal system. But so far, on the empirical record, every other system looks worse. No other—not even medieval feudalism—has ever taken the impulse of the Christian gospel or the Jewish prophetic tradition so deeply into its own institutional structure. Those who would destroy it must make more accurate diagnoses than they yet have. They need first to show that they are not merely repeating, without thought, the conventional biases of the clerks.

ALBERT SHANKER

5. *Trade Unions Strengthen Capitalism*

PAUL JOHNSON'S ESSAY presents something of a paradox. It is a paean to the glories of capitalism, a system that may constitute, in Johnson's words, "the greatest single blessing ever bestowed on humanity." But it is also rather like a dirge—a plaintive prophecy that capitalism is doomed. To be sure, this is not Johnson's conclusion. Capitalism will survive, he says, because of its "intrinsic virtues as a system for generating wealth and promoting freedom."

Johnson's original audience of bankers and businessmen may have derived some encouragement from his clarion call to "stop apologizing and go on the ideological offensive." But if they were encouraged they shouldn't have been. If they took seriously his analysis of the threats to capitalism, they could only conclude that the offensive he called for would have about as much chance of success as the Charge of the Light Brigade. Of these five "threats," three are derived from institutions that are pivotal and indispensable in any modern industrial society: the university, the unions, and the government. The university, according to Johnson, threatens to become the "graveyard" of capitalism—indeed, of Western individualism as well. The unions "undermine the performance of industrial capitalism as a wealth-creating system." Big government and capital-

ALBERT SHANKER *is president of the American Federation of Teachers and a vice-president of the AFL-CIO. He writes frequently in magazines and education journals and has a weekly column in the "New York Times."*

ism are, he says, "natural and probably irreconcilable enemies."

Continuing in this melancholy vein, Johnson portrays the anti-growth environmentalist movement—or rather, to use his term, the "ecology panic"—as "a potent destructive force." So potent and destructive is it, in fact, that it actually "played a crucial role in persuading" the OPEC cartel to quadruple oil prices, a move that "robbed Western capitalism of its tremendous élan, perhaps for good." In case there are still a few rays of hope left in his audience, Johnson administers the *coup de grâce* by introducing the fifth and most lethal threat: Communism. If the United States bows out of the arms race with the Soviet Union, we must then expect to see the Communists "hard at work winding up industrial capitalism and free enterprise all over the world."

Suddenly, having finished this relentlessly pessimistic analysis, Johnson launches into a short pep talk about the possibilities of victory if the friends of capitalism "go on the ideological offensive." Here we have an example of extreme voluntarism: all the objective factors indicate that we are doomed, but we will prevail if only we will go out there and fight.

Fortunately for everyone concerned, capitalists and non-capitalists alike, reality is considerably different from Johnson's picture of it. Capitalism is neither so mortally threatened nor so exquisitely virtuous as Johnson would have us believe. It faces serious difficulties, most of them of its own making, none of them insurmountable.

First, the university. Concerning the hostility of the intellectual class to capitalism, Johnson adds nothing to what Joseph Schumpeter said decades earlier. The difference is that Schumpeter understood how the capitalist class itself created and subsidized its intellectual enemies, and even allowed itself to be educated by them. Schumpeter had no answer to this problem, but at least he recognized it as a genuine dilemma rooted in the contradiction between a coldly rationalistic system of production and human impulses that continue to be "sub- or super-rational."

Without minimizing the problem of the intellectual "opposition culture," I think we should keep it in perspective. In the first place, it is not clear how capitalism can survive *without* the university, which is the training ground for an increasingly professionalized work force. The vast increase in higher education, made possible by the G.I. Bill of Rights and other forms of public loans and grants, has sustained the extraordinary growth of production that we have enjoyed since the Second World War. Higher education is, in a sense, the linchpin of American industrial genius, the factor chiefly responsible for making America the most technologically advanced and innovative country in the world.

Moreover, the university is hardly the hotbed of extremism that Johnson says it is. A survey of university faculty opinion, conducted in 1977 by Everett Carll Ladd, Jr., and Seymour Martin Lipset, found that 81 per cent of faculty members in this country agreed that "the private business system in the United States, for all its flaws, works better than any other system devised for advanced industrial society." Compared to the attitudes of the general population, faculty attitudes were only slightly more liberal, and the great majority of faculty members (75 per cent, as opposed to only 67 per cent for the general population) characterized themselves as "moderate," "somewhat liberal," or "somewhat conservative." Overall it is hard to accept Johnson's description of the university as the graveyard of Western individualism and enterprise.

Nor is it true that the government is the irreconcilable enemy of the free-enterprise economy. On the contrary, the prevailing system throughout the West is the mixed economy, consisting of both public and private sectors. Only very extreme conservatives still deny, at this late date, that the orderly working of the market economy requires substantial government intervention. The mixed economy may not be "the greatest single blessing ever bestowed on humanity," but it is certainly the most successful economic arrangement ever devised.

Of course, the system must be kept in proper balance. Too much government is as bad as too little government. But this is a far cry from saying that the public and private sectors are fundamentally antagonistic to each other. The relationship is one of interdependence. The conservative critics of government intervention never object when government intervenes to assist business, but they do object when government regulates business activities in such areas as plant safety, product safety, and pollution—activities that affect the health and welfare of workers and the general public.

The environmentalist movement often resorts to government regulation of business to achieve its goals, and it is true that there are powerful anti-growth tendencies in this movement. But there is also a strong tendency among businessmen to resist necessary environmental reforms on the pretext that they will restrict economic growth. In the United States, safety and health regulations passed during the last decade have significantly reduced plant accidents, pollution from carbon monoxide and sulfur dioxide, and water pollution. It is true that safety, health, and environmental regulations have added to the cost of production, though not to the degree often claimed by business. (The total economic cost of these regulations has been less than the price inflation caused by the regulations of market-fixing agencies such as the Interstate Commerce Commission—regulations to which business has not objected.) But on the other side of the ledger are lives saved and, secondarily, medical bills reduced.

How are we to judge the degree of environmental regulation that is desirable? Society needs both growth *and* clean air, and a sensible policy would aim at achieving an optimum mix. But if environmentalists often show little regard for economic growth and jobs, businessmen often act as if the only factor worth considering were the cost of production.

The one institution with a balanced approach to both growth and environmentalism is the labor movement—the fourth item in Johnson's demonology. It is also the one institution to take a balanced view of a whole series of issues that have sharply divided our society. Take, for instance, the debate over production and distribution. At the risk of oversimplifying, it may be said that the Right generally wants high production at the expense of fair distribution, while the Left would reverse this preference. Labor wants both, which is not surprising, since higher production means more jobs while fairer distribution means a higher standard of living.

Unions are not just the natural result of capitalism in a democratic society; they are absolutely essential for economic stability and the successful functioning of the entire system. The gains achieved by unions, both at the bargaining table and through legislation, have put a demand floor beneath the economy. This is the main reason why the economic slowdown of recent years has been much more moderate than the collapse during the Great Depression of the 1930s. Unions have also provided for the effective participation of workers in the economic process. Without collective bargaining, there would be no means for the orderly resolution of those conflicts between labor and management that are an intrinsic part of our economic system. The alternative is the use of force and the growth of extremism and anarchy.

Johnson has obviously been affected by the bitter industrial disputes that have plagued Britain in recent years. But this hardly justifies his traveling across the Atlantic to spur business to resist a modest legislative change that would secure the proper enforcement of labor laws already on the books. I doubt whether Johnson was very familiar with the issues involved in the 1978 labor-law reform fight in Congress. He may not have been aware of the resort by business to harassment, intimidation, and endless litigation to prevent workers from organizing and to obstruct the enforcement of the law. That is all the more reason why he should have kept out of an American dispute and not lent his voice to an insidious campaign to deny workers the right of association guaranteed by law. For that, after all, was the issue: not forced unionization, which was how business misrepresented the issue, but the right of workers to choose whether or not they wanted to join a union. It seems hypocritical to deny that right and in the same breath to speak of the virtues of individualism and to extol the freedom of the worker "to sell his labor and skills in the open market."

At issue is not just the future of capitalism but the well-being of democratic society and its security. I have spoken of the contribution of unions to economic stability and growth and to the overall security and standard of living of individual citizens. They are also the one mass-based institution that has supported democratic policies abroad as well as at home. There is a deep and rich anti-totalitarian tradition among American unions, a tradition that is based upon a commitment to democracy and free trade unionism. Does Johnson think that weakening unions would somehow strengthen our capacity to resist Communism? If so, he should think again. The effect instead would be to weaken our country's resolve by fostering bitter, enervating social conflicts, the rise of extremism at both ends of the political spectrum, and the gradual erosion of both labor's strength and its democratic, anti-Communist spirit.

Johnson advocates the defense of capitalism as the best way to oppose Communism. But surely he knows that capitalist businessmen have done more to help Communism, through the transfer of capital and technology, than any other group in Western society. He implicitly admits this when he says that "both the Communist world and the Third World are parasitical upon industrial capitalism for their growth technology." This is true, and the consequences have been devastating, at least with regard to the growth of Soviet military power. In this respect capitalism has been incredibly short-sighted, pursuing profit even if it meant supplying our enemies with the rope to hang us.

Johnson should remember that it was not American business but American labor that gave a platform to Solzhenitsyn and Bukovsky. And it has also been labor, not business, that has been most consistently anti-Communist. In the major study of the transfer of Western technology to the Soviet Union, Antony Sutton, a conservative, reached the "surprising conclusion" that "organizations which are often thought to be somewhat socialist in character, such as cooperatives and trade unions, have consistently refused to have anything to do with the Soviet Union in the matter of credits, aid, trade, or technical assistance. . . . On the other hand, the industrial and financial elements in all Western countries have, in the final analysis, provided more assistance for the growth of the Soviet Union than any other group" (*Western Technology and Soviet Economic Development,* Vol. I, Hoover Institution Press, 1968).

I suggest that businessmen treat with caution the enthusiasm of those who change from radical socialists to staunch defenders of business. Is it possible that the views of such people are no more sound today than they were before? I think so.

The success of the American system has been largely a function of our pragmatism and our resistance to rigid ideological thinking. It would be ironic, to say the least, if such thinking were brought to our country from abroad under the guise of the defense of capitalism. I cannot see anything constructive resulting from the embrace by business of an ideology that sees business engaged in a life-and-death struggle against intellectuals, political leaders, and trade unionists. I think business leaders would ultimately find themselves more isolated and disoriented than they are now.

The problems our society faces are complex. Johnson touches on many of them: growth, energy, the environment, the welfare state, the threat to freedom posed by Communism, the alienation of youth, the failure of will among our leaders. Business leaders must be part of the solution to all these problems. But it would be self-deluding for them to think that they have all the answers, or that by becoming more defensive or more aggressive toward other groups they will somehow enhance their own or society's capacity for intelligent progress. Capitalism does have a future, not as one party to a deepening class and social conflict in the West, but as a partner in a pluralistic system whose strength lies in its continuing ability to innovate and to resolve conflicts through the democratic process.

If there is to be a new "ideological offensive," let it be on behalf of democracy. That kind of a campaign would have a unifying effect and, unlike the campaign for defending capitalism proposed by Johnson, would have a chance to succeed.

J. ROBERT NELSON

6. Capitalism: Blessing and Curse

PAUL JOHNSON'S DESCRIPTION OF THE astounding effects of industrial capitalism within two hundred years reminds us of other remarkable developments in this relatively brief period. Except for some realms of philosophy, religion, literature, and the arts—visual, auditory, and culinary—our present civilization is wholly different from that of the eighteenth century. He is probably correct in comparing the slums and peasants' hovels of Europe in that century to those in the poorest lands of the Southern Hemisphere today. In hundreds of respects our present world, whether brave or not, is certainly new. And for millions of people it is manifestly better in three broad categories—health, education, and welfare.

Johnson does not choose to argue that the capitalist economy had a great deal to do with the generally improved lot of countless human beings who, thanks to science and technology, will now live to maturity and old age. Before the advent of capitalism, utter poverty, malnutrition, and mortal diseases were common conditions; the primary question was not how to *enhance* life but how to *survive*. Industrial capitalism is sustaining growing numbers of human beings at a higher level of health and material well-being. No one can deny that this is largely the result of a sense of

J. ROBERT NELSON *is professor of theology at Boston University. He is active in the World Council of Churches and represents the American Academy of Arts and Sciences on the National Commission for UNESCO.*

individual worth, initiative, aspiration, and competition. These human qualities had for centuries been denied and suppressed in the common people. They were like white roots and stems found under flat rocks. The plants are alive, but barely so; only when they are uncovered and exposed to sunlight can they grow and develop color. The use of technology to make a profit on invested capital, encouraged by increasingly democratic political societies, was like the lifting of a heavy stone from Western Europe and America.

Johnson does not overstate the case for crediting capitalism—both the ideology and the economic system—for much of what the developed countries enjoy and take for granted. He could have extended the catalogue of its good influences. But he could also have noted the conditions and strictures that have been imposed upon the exuberant free enterprise of the nineteenth century. Government regulation, brought about by democratically elected legislatures, shows that citizens recognized dangers and evils inherent in that economic system. They have seen capitalism for what it is: both a blessing and a curse.

Perhaps this perception of paradox derives from the religious force usually associated with the rise of capitalism—Calvinism. To those most conscious of being God's elect and most obedient to his will is attributed the famous work ethic. But whether or not they were Calvinists, many of the early capitalists were indeed tirelessly industrious, thrifty, and imbued with a sense of rightness and destiny. How could they avoid believing that divine and benign Providence had given to the British the nearly inexhaustible natural resources of a world empire and to Americans the unexplored and as yet unexploited North American continent (though the new Jerusalem they felt called to build in the green lands of England and New England turned out to be more commercial than heavenly).

The same Providence that gave them resources and inspired resourcefulness also required justice and mercy. While the early capitalists, who could be described as "God-fearing," had a limited concept of what justice required, they did give expression to mercy through acts of philanthropy that partially expiated their sin of acquisitiveness. Many colleges, universities, libraries, museums, charitable institutions, and foundations owe their existence in large measure to the "plagued conscience" of Christian and Jewish capitalists.

But this was not enough to offset the ill effects on the population of economic control by large corporations. As the era of robber barons gave way to the era of big business, the necessity of government regulation was apparent. Implicit in the motivation for regulation was a biblical teaching: the same heart of man that rejoices in the blessings of prosperity remains wicked and exceedingly self-centered. If there is any truth in the saying that there was more Methodism than Marxism in the rise of British socialism, a similar observation about religious influence is appropriate to America's willingness to accept the Rooseveltian reforms that rendered fully obsolete the concept of *laissez-faire*.

Paul Johnson's discussion of the relation between government and business is inadequate. It is merely contentious to say that industrial capitalism and big government are irreconcilable enemies. He has a legitimate complaint against *excessive* controls by government, but he goes much further and appears to preclude *proper* controls. He implies that the only alternative to big government's power over the economy is no control at all.

His discussion of labor unions leads to a similarly erroneous conclusion: better none at all than what we have in Britain and America today. This is unfortunate, since many who are sympathetic with Johnson's opposition to Marxism and Communism cannot believe that our national government and labor unions are equally perilous to a good society.

His polemic against the false gods and false hopes of Communism certainly is justified; but it would be more compelling if he had shown that the outrages of which industrial capitalism stands accused are easily matched, or exceeded, by those in socialist countries. These have to do with three kinds of exploitation: human, international, and ecological. Critics and dedicated opponents of capitalism have convincing reasons for faulting the corporate powers of free (or nearly free) enterprise. Countless workers and their dependents have suffered abuses and deprivations; natural resources of less developed countries have been pillaged for the profit of the rich ones; our air, water, and soil have been polluted. Johnson is not disposed to mention these vulnerable aspects of capitalist societies, which are the prime targets of both the academic Marxists and the pamphleteers. Neither does he admit the extent to which industrial capitalism is linked with, and dependent upon, the European and American production of military hardware and all the ancillary materials and services useful only to defense and warfare. Remembering that it was a representative of capitalist interests, President Eisenhower, whose last testament was a grave warning against the "military-industrial complex," we may find all the less convincing Johnson's generalization that industry and government are natural enemies.

These arguments can readily be turned back against Marxist apologists for socialist and Communist states and economies. When one thinks only of the Soviet Union's control over Eastern Europe, its expropriation of raw materials and manufactured products for itself, its spoliation of the natural environment, and its abysmal record of human degradation and oppression, it is obvious that the Communist pot has no basis for calling the capitalist kettle black. To make these points would strengthen the case for capitalism as an imperfect yet preferable mode of production and distribution.

Johnson's animosity toward what he calls the "ecolobby" is excessive and perplexing. He gives the impression that he believes in industry's willingness and capability to care for the plundered planet by itself. Evidence abounds to show that this is an ill-founded belief—a point dramatized in March 1979 when the world turned horrified eyes on the Three Mile Island nuclear power reactor near Harrisburg, Pennsylvania. Although its malfunction and threatened explosion of radioactive materials were brought under control with no human death or injury, the catastrophic possibility was enough to negate such blithe cases for developing nuclear power as Johnson's.

Though his style is engaging and articulate, Johnson falls short of making a satisfying apologia for industrial capitalism in our time. This is disappointing. There is merit in his trenchant observations about Marxists. He is right to point to the erosion of both the ideologically informed will and the political conditions that can make capitalism work as it should— i.e., for the common good. Not socialism but social mutuality and human solidarity must now determine our evaluation of any economic or political system.

EUGENE J. McCARTHY

7. Corporations Have Corrupted Capitalism

LITTLE CAN BE SAID AGAINST Paul Johnson's case for the productive power of capitalism, whether a particular capitalist's motivation was to amass wealth (as the economist Carl Snyder observed years ago, "Deep as are our prejudices against avarice and greed, it cannot be denied that they have been great forces for the building of the modern economic world"), to demonstrate personal power and achievement (as in the case of empire-builders like Andrew Carnegie and James Hill), or to contribute to human welfare. Today the theoretical challenge, if it can properly be called that, is not to traditional capitalism but to capitalism as it is manifested in the corporation.

When economists began to write about the economics of "imperfect competition," they signaled the end of the pure economics of Adam Smith and of capitalism. Today nearly 80 per cent of the productive activity in the United States is controlled by corporate organizations operating under charters granted by the states. These corporations are not free, competing entities but institutions given special privileges and advantages over individuals by legal social decision.

James Kent, in his *Commentaries on American Law,* published early in the nineteenth century, observed that "the number of charters of incorpo-

---

EUGENE J. McCARTHY, *former representative and senator from Minnesota and a former professor of politics, history, and literature, is a syndicated columnist and poet. He is the author of ten books.*

ration" was increasing in the United States with a disturbing rapidity. "We are multiplying in this country to an unparalleled extent the institution of corporations," he said, "and giving them a flexibility and variety of purpose unknown to the Roman or to the English law."

Competition does not rule the economy of the United States today. More and more, differences between the largest corporations and the government are settled not within a framework of law but by negotiation. For example, when Du Pont was ordered to divest itself of General Motors stock some seventeen years ago, the existing antitrust laws and penalties were not applied. Congress passed special legislation to work out the transition. In much the same way, the taxation of insurance companies and of oil companies has been settled by negotiation rather than by the application of public judgment and law.

The government's dealings with the steel industry in recent years demonstrate the same relationship. During the Korean War, when President Truman tried to prevent a slowdown in steel production by issuing an executive order to take over the industry, the independence of the industry was sustained by the Supreme Court.

Subsequent challenges to the industry were handled differently. The Kennedy administration responded to a major increase in the price of steel not by attempting to apply the existing law or by executive order but by public denunciation and, according to some reports, by midnight calls from the FBI to steel-company officials.

In the Johnson administration, the presidents of steel companies were called to the White House for "jawboning" sessions, generally approved by the press and politicians. The message was not that competition, the free economy, and the law of supply and demand should be allowed to prevail but that prices should be kept down. The steel-company officers, champions of free enterprise and of capitalism, surrendered, seeming to accept the idea that if prices were fixed in Pittsburgh, that would be an "action in restraint of trade." It was rather as if an English king had called in the nobles and said: "If you agree to these things in my presence, you will be able to do them. But if you agree to them among yourselves in Wales, you will be in deep trouble."

It has been suggested that the U.S. government seek the equivalent of diplomatic representation on the boards of major corporations, especially those that are deeply involved in foreign business and finance.

What we have in America is not a free, competitive, capitalistic system but a kind of corporate feudalism. In the feudal system, according to a schoolboy's definition, everyone belonged to someone and everyone else belonged to the king. In the modern order, nearly every worker belongs to some corporation, and everyone else belongs to the government, federal, state, or local.

A corporately controlled economy has left us with a situation in which there is widespread poverty, serious unemployment, the wasting of resources, shortages, and inflation. The corporation is not wholly responsible for these conditions. Undoubtedly outside policy or forces, such as war and government fiscal policies and regulations, have an adverse affect on the general economy and specifically on some institutions and businesses.

The concept of the corporation as an instrument for the conduct of business and financial affairs is a valid one. But it is a concept that must prove its vitality in practice. If the corporation is to be privileged by law, as it is now, and if it is to control most of the powers on which the material well-being of the nation depends, then it must become more effective and more responsible, both socially and economically.

PAUL CRAIG ROBERTS

8. The Failure
of the Intellectuals

UNLESS PAUL JOHNSON WAS AN UNUSUAL editor of the *New Statesman,* his essay signifies yet another defection from the anti-capitalist ranks and is itself evidence that, contrary to what he says, capitalism has *not* lost "the intellectual and moral battle." People simply haven't "voted with their feet" in favor of collectivism, and many intellectuals who once voted with their minds have since changed them. Those who still keep alive the collectivist make-believe do so from a safe and comfortable distance. Shirley MacLaine has not emigrated to China, nor George McGovern to Vietnam. Not a single admiring journalist has chucked America for Cuba, and Noam Chomsky is still at M.I.T., feeding well from the capitalist endowment. What more crushing defeat can the leftist litany suffer than the fact that no one is fleeing from racist, sexist, polluted, capitalist America? There are no American boat people. There are not even any black South African boat people.

No, capitalism has not lost the intellectual and moral battle. It has won it hands down. But the victory may not be relevant.

People in the West have little historical consciousness, and unless they are practicing politicians, they assume that truth, justice, and morality,

PAUL CRAIG ROBERTS *is associate editor of the editorial page of the "Wall Street Journal" and senior research fellow at the Hoover Institute. He has taught economics, served as an advisor on Capitol Hill, and written two books and numerous articles.*

which mean widely different things to different people, are nonetheless powerful historical forces that one must have on one's side. Thus: we gave up in Vietnam and betrayed our allies there to get in step with morality. Even many patriots who are still fuming about the student protesters of the 1960s believe we lost that war because we were short on morality. They simply can't conceive of any other explanation.

Marx and Lenin, on the other hand, believed such ideas to be bourgeois illusions. In their view, truth, justice, and morality are only masks that veil class interests and the drive to power. Violence, not morality, mediates between different interests. "Communists preach no morality at all," Marx declared characteristically. Engels found moral theories "as powerless as Kant's categorical imperative." "The levers of historical progress," he said, are "the evil passions of men, greed, and imperiousness." Lenin explicitly developed this doctrine of violence. Listen as he says: "The scientific concept of dictatorship means neither more nor less than unlimited power, resting directly on force, not limited by anything, not restricted by any laws, nor any absolute rules. Nothing else but that."

There is no evidence that Lenin's followers were shocked by this doctrine or that they discarded it upon his death. Rather, they seem to have taken it for granted. For example, in 1928 Grigori Pyatakov, later a victim of the doctrine, recognized and approved it: "According to Lenin, the Communist party is based on the principle of coercion, which doesn't recognize any limitations or inhibitions. And the central idea of this principle of boundless coercion is not coercion by itself but the absence of any limitation whatsoever—moral, political, and even physical."

This doctrine has a long tradition, and it has survived its practice by Stalin, Mao, and Pol Pot. The Hungarians ran up against it in 1956 and the Czechoslovakians in 1968. Dissidents in Russia run into it today when they appeal to the constitution and find that the party, instead, is supreme.

I am not saying that there is no such thing as morality—just that moral victories over people who rely on power might not count for much. How do you appeal to the good will of people who don't believe in it?

The problem is not with capitalism or any shortage of moral victories but with intellectuals who adopt an entirely critical posture toward their own society. Under the barrage of debunking and unmasking, the victories go unrecorded. But while intellectuals denounce, illegal aliens affirm.

Paul Johnson rightly notes that many people today are engaged in criticizing capitalism. One reason might be that the state ensures many of these critics a good living. The main achievement of the critics of capitalism has been to open up vast opportunities for the growth of government. Any social scientist who can discover a social problem that can be parlayed into a new federal program is set for life. The academic intellectual's distaste for capitalism may simply reflect his symbiotic relationship with big government: he is subsidized by the state to discover social imperfections, because each imperfection justifies an increase in state power to correct the imperfection. Many of the "moral critics" of capitalism might simply be well-paid agents of the state in disguise.

Nevertheless, if all the state's hired hands in our midst were arrested for the fraud of which they are guilty, there would still be a problem. Khieu Samphan, Pol Pot's predecessor, learned his Marxism at the Sorbonne, where his thesis stressed social purification at any cost. Where does such fierceness come from?

I believe it flows from an inconsistency in the intellectual foundation of Western civilization. The Enlightenment had two results that combine to produce a destructive formula. On the one hand, Christian moral fervor was secularized, which produced demands for the moral perfection of society. On the other hand, modern science hammered epistemology into a critical philosophical positivism that is skeptical of the reality of moral motives. From the one we get moral indignation, and from the other, moral skepticism. How can two such disparate tendencies be reconciled?

The answer seems to be that this inconsistent combination is held together by a joint attack on existing society. One pre-empts existing society's defense, while the other focuses moral indignation against it. Together they support a social and political dynamism that seeks to achieve progress by remaking society.

Affirmations of society's achievements run into this dynamism, which mows them down with skepticism and indignation. People who are motivated by moral purposes find that they have a safe outlet only in accusations of immorality against existing society, and the West's morality becomes immanent in attacks on itself.

The problem with the West is that its intellectuals are victimized by the contradiction in their intellectual heritage. Very few of them can rise above it. Capitalism has not failed, but the intellectuals have.

Although I am not more joyful over one returning sinner than ten just men, and although it may have taken Paul Johnson longer to return than it should have, I am glad to see one fewer Western intellectual preparing the world for the ravages of ruthless power by insanely denouncing his own heritage.

JAMES CONE

9. Capitalism Means Property Over Persons

SOME PERSPECTIVES DIFFER SO radically from my own that I hardly know where to begin in responding to them. Having read Paul Johnson's address several times, I still find it hard to believe that he can so uncritically support capitalism in the face of the vast human suffering arising from it. How should I respond to a point of view that seems completely insensitive to many human factors that I regard as important?

I will focus my comments on the *selective* character of Paul Johnson's argument for industrial capitalism. Because I am a black American whose value system has been shaped in the historical context of an oppressed people's struggle for justice, I cannot avoid evaluating a given sociopolitical perspective in terms of how it helps or hinders that struggle. If one takes the general principle of "justice for the poor" as the criterion, Johnson's apology for capitalism is completely unconvincing. He shows little or no concern for oppressed humanity in Europe, the United States, and the Third World. It is as if they do not exist.

When a people's existence is not recognized, it means that their suffering is considered to have no bearing on the value of a given political system if that system continues to serve the interests of those for whom it was created. That was why white North Americans could speak of the United

JAMES CONE *is professor of systematic theology at Union Theological Seminary in New York. He is the author of several books on theology and politics, including "A Black Theology of Liberation."*

States as the "land of the free" while they held Africans as slaves. Similarly, Paul Johnson can speak of capitalism as "the greatest single blessing ever bestowed on humanity" even though the vast majority of people have been victimized by it. He seems to be saying that as long as the white European and American ruling classes benefit from the profits of capitalism, its shortcomings in contributing toward the liberation of the poor from their poverty cannot count significantly against its value for humanity. Value is defined in terms of material profit for the rich, not economic and political structures for the benefit of all. It is this implication that makes his viewpoint reprehensible from my ethical perspective.

For whom does Johnson speak and for what purpose? I think the answer is obvious. He speaks for the haves and not the have-nots, for the rich and not the poor, for whites and not blacks, for the United States and Europe and not for Asia, Africa, and Latin America. His purpose is to show that recent threats to industrial capitalism arise not from the masses of people but rather from university intellectuals, trade unions, big government, ecology campaigners, and the Soviet Union. This selective focus and his caricature of the opponents of capitalism define the character of his address; he thereby limits the possibility of genuine dialogue with anyone whose perspective has been shaped by solidarity with the victims of industrial capitalism.

Johnson's defense of industrial capitalism centers on its ability to produce an "unprecedented annual growth rate" in Europe and North America. Aside from Japan, there is no mention in this connection of any country in the Third World. Nor does he say anything about the relation between the wealth of Europe and the United States and the poverty in Asia, Africa, and Latin America. Is he suggesting that this wealth is in no way connected with and dependent upon slavery and colonization in the Third World? Because the examples he gives of the value of industrial capitalism are almost exclusively limited to Europe and the United States, I am particularly interested in how he would explain the huge gap between the rich and the poor on both continents, but especially in Asia, Africa, and Latin America. And why does he not mention that though the United States has only 6 per cent of the world's population, it consumes over 30 per cent of the world's natural resources?

I contend that capitalism is under threat not because it has received a bad press from university intellectuals, ecology campaigners, and trade-union people, nor because of big government or even the outside danger of the Soviet Union, but because the so-called free-enterprise system is not free at all; it is actually controlled by multinational corporations.

I agree with Johnson that the capitalist economies of the United States and Europe have produced a lot of wealth. But I also know that the masses of people on both continents do not receive their just share of that wealth. While legislators in the United States enact laws almost yearly that appear to guarantee a fairer distribution, statistics show that the very rich still control a hugely disproportionate amount of the nation's wealth. This rich ruling class makes up only 0.5 per cent of the population but controls over one-fourth of the nation's privately held wealth and yearly income, including 50-86 per cent of all corporate stock (see Jonathan Turner and Charles Staines, *Inequality: Privilege and Poverty in America,* Goodyear, 1976).

When these economic factors are set in a racial context, the injustice is even more striking. Blacks and other U.S. minorities are especially victimized, because their color is an additional factor contributing to the economic injustice inflicted upon them. Aside from the small minority of black professionals who are needed to create the appearance of equality in the United States, blacks and other ethnic minorities are the last hired and often the first fired. Their unemployment rate is always four to ten times higher than that of whites. They are forced to live in urban ghettoes with no real opportunity to participate in shaping the laws that affect their community.

People who share Paul Johnson's perspective like to delude themselves into thinking that the poor enjoy living in poverty. They nourish this delusion by spending most of their time talking to rich capitalists and their supporters rather than to the poor. Yet they like to claim that they know what the poor think. What they label as the "poor" perspective is nothing but the reinforcement of the ruling-class point of view. In the United States I have met many white people who share Johnson's viewpoint. They were plentiful during the civil-rights struggle in the 1950s and '60s, and today they are even more vocal in advocating the essential justice of the American capitalist system. When poor black people, during the 1960s, reacted in violent rebellion against intolerable economic conditions, white oppressors simply attributed such behavior to the influence of outside agitators and gave a military response that left many blacks dead in the streets.

Economic conditions in U.S. cities are no better today for the masses of blacks than they were in the 1960s. But I am sure that urban police departments are better prepared for any disturbance that black people's poverty may motivate them to create. People who share Paul Johnson's perspective seem to be more concerned about eliminating social unrest through the power of the police than about eliminating the economic conditions that create the unrest.

Paul Johnson either is unaware of the gross injustices created by capitalism or has simply chosen to ignore them. If he thinks that the growth of megalopolises all over the world is evidence of a popular endorsement of capitalism, he is grossly mistaken. Poor people migrate to urban centers because they are trying to survive in a situation of maldistributed wealth. Whatever else may be said about the wealth that capitalism generates in the United States, poor blacks and other minorities do not benefit from it.

When capitalism's wealth is viewed in an international context, the injustice it creates appears even greater. The wealth of Europe and the United States is directly determined by the poverty of the people of Asia, Africa, and Latin America. This is the historical significance of slavery and colonization, which today are continued in the economic domination of the Third World by the United States and Europe. Despite the Western world's verbal defense of human rights and freedom, its continued economic and military support of the dictator governments of South Africa, South Korea, Chile, and many other states completely invalidates what it says.

Although I am a Christian whose ethical perspective is derived primarily from that tradition, I do not need to appeal to Christianity to demonstrate the gross immorality of economic arrangements defined by capitalism. One needs only to be sensitive to human beings and their right to life, liberty, and the pursuit of happiness to question seriously what Paul Johnson advocates. Capitalism is a system that clearly values property more than persons. That is why it is losing the moral and intellectual battle. And perhaps it is why Paul Johnson appeals to material statistics as evidence for the inherent value of capitalism rather than to the quality of life it makes possible for all people.

RITA HAUSER

10. The Problem of Persistent Inequality

PAUL JOHNSON MAKES PLAIN THE historic benefits produced by the advent of modern capitalism, most particularly, freedom from the legal and personal restraints of feudalism, enhanced economic opportunity, and the potential for human development on a larger scale. He concludes, however, that these benefits are under sustained attack, principally by intellectuals, university leaders, and journalists. Indeed, he blames the expansion of higher education in the 1960s for the current assault on free enterprise, since it generated broad acceptance of Marxist ideology, student unrest, environmentalist movements seeking to thwart growth, and the like. He also points to the growth of interventionist government as a source of attack on the capitalist system.

All this is surely correct, but Johnson's approach is far too simplistic to explain the current widespread dissatisfaction with free enterprise.

Free enterprise made it possible to satisfy the material needs of many people. It produced an unprecedented level of affluence. But while more people than ever before were very well off, many were badly off in comparison. Some highly educated people believe that the capitalist system sets out deliberately to benefit some at the expense of others, and that only in this way can capitalism advance. Marxist opinions will therefore

RITA HAUSER *is a partner in the law firm of Stroock, Stroock, and Lavan in New York. She has represented the United States in a number of international organizations, including the U.N. Commission on Human Rights.*

always find support, for it is inherent in the uncontrolled operation of any free system that the results or benefits it produces will be unequal. Attempts are then made to control the system in order to provide more for the disadvantaged, and some form of welfare state begins to engraft itself onto the free-enterprise system, distorting it finally to the point where, as in Britain, it ceases to be truly productive of wealth.

The problem cannot be met by a return to unbridled free enterprise. Rather, the urgent need is to devise better ways of sharing the wealth without destroying the golden goose. This is a problem for lawyers, economists, and social theorists. No means of adjusting the system to perfection has yet been found. The United States, still experimenting, may now be at the point where further fine tuning of the system will lead into the British predicament. More government regulation and control would be likely to diminish productivity. Furthermore, whether the benefits to the disadvantaged from programs intended to help them have been proportionate to the costs involved is problematical; evidence suggests that bureaucracy, rather than the needy, is the main beneficiary of social programs.

Capitalism does have a future. But the way into that future is not to take Johnson's advice and go on the ideological offense. No system can save itself merely by teaching its history. Capitalism must conceive a means of distributing wealth that will satisfy the elementary requirements of justice. State capitalism is hardly the solution. Perhaps an imaginative tax policy, in place of the current welfare programs and most inequitable tax structure, is what is needed. So far, every serious attempt at tax reform has led to more loopholes for the privileged and more burdens for lawyers, accountants, and the like.

Capitalism's leaders, be they corporate chairmen or academic supporters, have failed to provide any creative thinking or leadership for resolving the problem of persistent inequality under capitalism. Unless there is progress in this area and the public begins to perceive capitalism as a system that can yield a satisfactory distribution of wealth, there will be little chance for private enterprise to overcome its current mood of defeatism. Mature capitalism needs to generate at least a reasonable minimum income for all who live under the system in order to sustain its own foundations.

JACK KEMP

11. Democratic Capitalism Needs More Democracy

HAS CAPITALISM A FUTURE? Not unless its advocates fundamentally improve their understanding of the system and how to make it work. My greatest doubts about the future of democratic capitalism arise not when I listen to its opponents but when I hear its supposed defenders talking about such things as the necessity of chronic recessions or the inevitability of inflation. People do "vote with their feet," as Paul Johnson says, and in the past people have voted overwhelmingly in favor of a system that could provide them with abundant economic opportunity and the security of stable prices. If the system is threatened today, it is not because people have suddenly been fooled into voting against their own interests; it is threatened because the people's needs and aspirations are no longer being fulfilled.

The threats to democratic capitalism outlined by Johnson, serious as they may be, were originally the results rather than the causes of the faltering performance of the system. Capitalism's adverse fortunes in the intellectual battle, the ecological panic, the growth of government, the rising power of special-interest groups, even the increasing threat from without— all are features of a stagnant or contracting economy. When there is less opportunity and employment, there will be more human needs that must be satisfied, by the government if not by the private economy; hence the

JACK KEMP *is a congressman from New York, a leading advocate of tax-rate reduction, and the second most famous alumnus from the Buffalo Bills football team.*

growth of government. When advocates of economic growth fail to achieve it, those redistributionists who always seem to be waiting in the wings have an appeal they would not have in a prosperous, growing economy; hence the doubtful outcome of the intellectual battle. In a contracting economy, life becomes a "zero-sum game"—one in which one person or group can gain only if another loses. People are forced to spend more of their time organizing to protect their interests and less time in productive activity; hence the proliferation of special-interest groups. When the economy falters, there are always some latter-day Malthusians who conclude that the earth is running out of everything; hence the ecological panic. Even the external threat from the opponents of democratic capitalism is increased when our ability to provide for both adequate security and necessary social programs is reduced. Our weakness is provocative; our opponents become bold and gain international respect.

I believe the fault lies with the political leadership rather than with the democratic political economy or the people—which are really the same thing. The free economic market is as much a democratic expression of people's desires as is the political marketplace in the voting booth. The distinguishing feature of capitalism is not the institution of incorporation but the guarantee of certain economic and political freedoms. Capitalism has a strong bias toward continuous economic growth because it permits people—individuals—to act upon the natural desire to improve their own condition and that of their families. The *Fortune* 500 corporations account for only a fraction of the nation's economic growth. Most growth comes from enterprises that are on their way from being someone's better idea to joining the *Fortune* 500. Most new jobs, new technology, and growth in the United States come from small businesses that begin with individuals. When the efforts of those individuals are rewarded, we see economic growth. When the government drives an unnecessary wedge between effort and reward, growth diminishes, and so does the support of those people who are "voting with their feet."

But this is not to say that the solution is to do away with government. The state is as unlikely to wither away into a libertarian utopia as into a Marxist utopia. As the guarantor of economic and political freedoms, the government is necessary to the proper functioning of democratic capitalism. It provides external defense, maintains a stable currency, performs necessary regulation, and provides other essential public services. People willingly pay taxes and submit to regulation as long as the public benefits justify the costs. But when the government takes too much from them, individual effort is discouraged.

The government's overtaxation or overregulation hurts even the government. When you tax something—and regulations are a sort of tax—you get less of that thing. When you tax work, savings, investment, production, and enterprise, there is less of all those things left to tax. At some point, increasing the tax and regulatory burden is subject to the law of diminishing returns. Under democratic capitalism, that point—the degree to which the government interferes in the democratic economic marketplace—is determined democratically in the political marketplace.

It has been demonstrated convincingly (see Jude Wanniski's *How the World Works*) that the economic upheavals of this century have been caused primarily by tax, regulatory, or monetary policy blunders by the government—blunders that excessively expanded the government's wedge between effort and reward. And the people responded to the decreased incentive each time by voting "with their feet" and with their ballots.

Our two periods of greatest prosperity since the First World War were initiated by economic strategies that increased individual and business incentives and maintained a stable currency. Treasury secretary Andrew Mellon presided over such a program under conservative Republican presidents Harding and Coolidge in the 1920s, and President Kennedy, a moderate Democrat, followed low-tax, free-trade, hard-currency policies in the early 1960s.

The post–World War I recession was caused primarily by an attempt to pay off the vast war debt by keeping tax rates at prohibitive wartime levels. The Crash of 1929 and the Great Depression that bottomed out in 1933 were largely caused by the drastic, protectionist Smoot-Hawley Tariff and Herbert Hoover's attempt to balance the budget in the ensuing recession by raising income tax rates 150 per cent. The 1950s were also a time of chronic recession, in part because tax rates were kept once again at wartime levels that extracted as much as ninety-one cents from a dollar of income. In the past decade we have seen two recessions caused by increases in the government's tax wedge, aggravated by dislocations caused by government price controls, especially on energy production, and inflamed by a continual devaluation of the dollar that, with a steeply progressive tax code, amounts to a perpetual increase in the tax rate.

Each of the recession-fostering mistakes amounted to meddling in the democratic nature of the marketplace, either by placing excessive burdens on individuals or by interfering in their free choice. Yet at least since the Great Depression, government policymakers have justified their actions by asserting that what failed was the system of democratic capitalism itself rather than government policy. They embraced new economic theories— Keynesianism and monetarism—that are based on the decidedly undemocratic notion that to get people to engage in economic activity you have to fool them.

Keynesians argue that the way to encourage economic growth is to create a budget deficit, usually through government spending. The government borrows money and issues bonds that it promises to repay with the receipts from future taxation. In other words, people are supposed to be fooled into trading their labor for bonds and not realize that they will be taxed in the future for the cost of the bonds, plus interest. *Monetarists* argue that people work for "money" rather than for the things that money can buy. By increasing the supply of money, they say, the government can fool people into accepting each newly devalued dollar at full value (at least until they discover the deception and demand more dollars).

Neither Keynesian nor monetarist theory allows for the possibility that people are smarter than government policymakers. We have observed the spectacular failure of both of these economic models in the past decade, as our economy has become mired in "stagflation" despite an enormous increase in public indebtedness and the money supply.

There is no mystery about why we had prosperity and price stability in the 1920s and the 1960s, and no reason why we cannot have them again. What is required is nothing more or less than heeding the economic lessons of history. When you tax something, you get less of that thing. When you create too many units of currency, each unit loses value. This does not mean that we have to do away with the safety net of social-welfare programs, which has been erected to protect people from the economic shocks that result from the tinkering of policymakers. But the fact that a safety net is desirable does not mean that it should always be full. Transfer programs should help people get on their feet again.

Has capitalism a future? History shows us nothing inevitable about the decline of a great civilization—and I consider this to be one of them. The golden age may be long or short; it ends only when the leaders forget what made that civilization great. Democratic capitalism has a future to the extent that its leaders become more democratic in both their economics and their politics.

HERMAN KAHN

12. Social Limits to Economic Growth

PAUL JOHNSON'S HISTORICAL OBSERVATIONS are generally sound, as are many of his comments on the current state of the world. I agree that the industrial revolution, with its accompanying sustained economic growth, technological advancement, and increasing affluence, is a unique product of Western culture and capitalist institutions. But the tremendous economic growth of the last two centuries is not likely to continue. Indeed, our analyses strongly indicate that the current slowing in the growth of the world's gross product, while affected by short and medium cyclical conditions, probably also reflects a long-term trend—indeed, we may not see a sustained 5 per cent growth rate (such as occurred between 1950 and 1973) again for a very long time, if ever.

That a peak occurs should not be surprising. The industrial revolution caused an apparent exponential growth. A simple projection of exponential growth rates leads to an absurd anticipated standard of living ($1.4 million gross product per person, in 1978 dollars, by the year 2200).

Failure to swallow such numbers with a grain of salt has led many latter-day Malthusians to predict disaster. They see the exponential growth of population, consumption of food and raw materials, and gross world product continuing until the carrying capacity of the earth is exceeded. Apparent

HERMAN KAHN, *a physicist, economist, and social analyst, is cofounder and director of the Hudson Institute. His many books cover a wide range of topics, from military affairs to economic development.*

exponential growth rates do occur in nature, as any biologist will confirm. But they don't last long. And the limits are as likely to be set by the animal equivalent of social limits to growth as by scarcity of food or uncontrolled pollution—though these occur, too.

Most of us at the Hudson Institute believe that limits to growth are now manifesting themselves in the world economy but that these are almost all social rather than physical—and are likely to remain so. In particular, long before we reach a long-term multiple resource or pollution crisis, the consequences of affluence will slow economic growth rates. That this may have already happened is indicated by one important variable: world population growth. Many forecasters assumed that this would continue at an exponential rate. Actually it probably peaked at about 2 per cent in the early or mid 1960s. Growth of the gross world product seems to have peaked at roughly 5 per cent in the early 1970s and is unlikely to reach that level again for any sustained period. A dramatic tapering off in both variables can be expected around the year 2000.

Fifteen new social emphases threaten to slow down or even stop economic growth in the affluent capitalist countries:

1. *Selective Risk Avoidance:* innovators, entrepreneurs, and businessmen generally must bear not only all risks but also the burden of proof, as if only they and not society as well benefited from their profits and efforts.

2. *Localism* ("ins" vs. "outs"): no local disturbance or risks are accepted because of the needs of the larger society.

3. *Comfort, Safety, Leisure, and Health Regulations:* often mandated by government regulation—and sometimes approaching "health and safety fascism."

4. *Protection of Environment and Ecology:* often at almost any cost to the economy or other programs.

5. *Loss of Nerve, Will, Optimism, Confidence, and Morale:* at least about economic progress and technological advancement.

6. *Public Welfare and Social Justice:* life must be made "fair"; equality of result, not of opportunity; justice should not be blind.

7. *Happiness and Hedonism:* as explicit and direct goals in life.

8. *General Anti-Technology, Anti-Economic-Development, and Anti-Middle-Class Attitudes:* although many in the "small is better" and "limits-to-growth" movements believe we are quite poor and getting poorer, enormous resources can be allocated or great economic costs accepted to further points 1-7 above.

9. *Increasing Social Control and "Overall Planning" of the Economy:* but mostly with New Class values and attitudes and by "input-output theorists."

10. *Regulatory Attitudes That Are Opposed or Indifferent to the Success of Business:* the productivity and profitability of business are taken for granted.

11. *"Modern" Family and Social Values and a De-emphasis of Many Traditional (Survival and Square) Values.*

12. *Concern with Self:* often accompanied by an emphasis on mystic or transcendental attitudes and values, or expressions of the "me generation."

13. *New "Secular" Rites, Ceremonies, and Celebrations:* both against and instead of traditional ones.

14. *New Sources of Meaningful Status and Prestige.*

15. *Increasingly Political Distribution of National Income* (e.g., more emphasis on union bargaining, welfare, and egalitarianism, and less on market forces and claims of property and skills).

These new emphases can be a much more powerful source of slowing or halting growth than any genuine resource or pollution problems. They form the basis of the concept of the "social limits to growth," which can occur in at least two forms: what Paul Johnson calls "creeping stagnation," or a more or less "natural and innate" development that is largely voluntary and acceptable, reflecting the tendency that as societies get richer they want, for example, cleaner air and water and are willing to pay for them. The people are not willing to be inconvenienced for the sake of economic growth. They sacrifice economic growth for various concepts of "the good life." But the phrase "creeping stagnation" implies that many people do not even know what trade-offs are being made. Limits are accepted (or forced) accidentally, incompetently, or prematurely because of the excessive influence of narrow interest groups. If the public were better informed, it would often choose more economic growth and fewer social limits.

Whether the new limitations are voluntary or not, we should not lose sight of the fact that the past two hundred years of Western civilization have been extraordinary. Before the advent of Western culture no society had ever achieved sustained economic growth. Earlier societies failed to develop, not because they physically lacked capability for growth, but because they were overwhelmed by social limitations. From the grand perspective of recorded history, the tendency for Western society to accept social limits to growth is a return to normal.

Presumably, even dedicated proponents of growth would not oppose many of the new social limitations if they were designed properly, were implemented efficiently, and continued to show a reasonable regard for traditional objectives and values. When the majority of the people become relatively well off, a likely prospect, they will strongly tend to share in many of the values expressed in the fifteen new emphases; i.e., the social limitations caused by these may then be judged largely "natural and innate." It is in fact a matter of degree. Most Americans would support the allocating of 10-20,000 square miles, perhaps even more, for an Alaskan wildlife preserve. But most would find shocking, if not bizarre, the idea that one should set apart almost 200,000 square miles (the size of France, or twice the size of England, West Germany, or Japan); yet this seems likely to happen. Much of the pressure for such social limitations today is either improvident or elitist.

I do not agree with Johnson that "the free-enterprise idea is losing . . . the intellectual and moral battle," though it has certainly come close to doing so. There is now, almost worldwide, more than a hint of a "conservative renaissance," a return to traditional values and a greater reliance on market concepts—even in Communist countries. During the post-war period there was, in the wealthy capitalist countries, a much more rapid rate of growth in the public sector than in the private sector. But in most countries this situation has begun to improve. In the United States it has been reversed, and I believe it will soon be reversed in the United Kingdom. (I am writing this in May 1979, when Margaret Thatcher and the Conservative party have just taken office.) If so—and if such experiments as the Barre plan in France and an increasing emphasis on freer enterprise in several Latin American countries turn out to be successful—then the free-enterprise idea should be sustained for at least a while.

Johnson's comments about the "knowledge industry" are also misleading. There is no question that the creation, production, transfer, recording, retrieval, dissemination, and analysis of information is becoming the largest industry, or at least the most predominant activity, in the developed world. Nor is there any question that many activities of the media and the educational establishment are destructive. In particular, the miseducation of young students, ideologically and practically, is a central problem; but I scarcely think of this as being an essential aspect of the knowledge industry. Just the sheer increase in the number of people getting advanced education makes it likely that more people will lose their ties with reality and quite easily accept various types of anti-capitalist and anti-technological think-ing. However, it is probably appropriate to think of current student terror-ism in continental Europe and Japan as less a result of the expansion of higher education (even though this may have been an essential element in the process) and more an excessive reaction to the defeat of the totalitarian ideologies of Germany, Italy, and Japan and the corresponding "de-author-ization" of the older generation and its traditions and values.

I agree with Johnson's discussion of the "ecological panic," but it must be seen as part of a general and pervasive social process. I also agree with his comments on the growth of government (though direct excessive growth is more prevalent in Europe and Canada than in the United States and Japan, while the growth of regulation is much worse in the United States than in Western Europe.) But all this may be checked or reversed, at least for the time being, by the "conservative renaissance."

Finally, I agree with Johnson that the continuation of recent trends in trade unions and the U.S.-Soviet military balance would mean our destruc-tion. But, as Johnson noted, it is not likely that the British style of trade unions will become worldwide, though unions can be bad in almost all democratic countries. And in national defense, the Carter administration, responding reluctantly to pressure, is moving to improve the balance of forces. In fact this program started in the Ford administration.

Johnson closes with this paragraph:

> Those who wish to maintain the capitalist system must endeavor to teach the world a little history. They must remind it, and especially the young, that though man's achievements are great, they are never as solid as they look. If man makes the wrong choice, there is always another Dark Age waiting for him round the corner of time.

We must indeed teach the young more history. But we have no reason to be quite so gloomy. The world is so technologically advanced, so capable of dealing with problems—there is so much economic surplus—that it is quite difficult to create a worldwide dark age by mistakes in policy, even if they are horrendous. With extraordinary bad luck, or an almost incredible level of mismanagement, it might be done. For the last decade or two, many influential and powerful elites practically, if unintentionally, did their best to wreck the United States. They left unpleasant legacies, but they failed. And what happened in the United States is not atypical. In general, the very good times that followed World War II are now being followed by an epoch of malaise—at least in wealthy nations (both Communist and market-oriented). These nations, neither sick nor well, are likely to go through some unsettling experiences that will cause them to restrain or even turn back the trends of the post-war period. It is most important that such attempts be given reasonable direction. The West will have company. South Korea, Brazil, Mexico, and others—even India—will probably succeed, at least to a degree, in carrying on their current relatively rapid rate of industrialization.